The Power of Your
Subconscious Mind
for Wealth
and Spirituality

Books by Joseph Murphy

How to Use the Laws of the Mind

Psychic Perception

Telepsychics

The Power of Your Subconscious Mind
for Wealth and Spirituality
(includes *Believe in Yourself, How to Prosper, Meditations &*
Affirmations, and *The Healing Power of Your Subconscious Mind*)

The Power of Your Subconscious Mind for Wealth and Spirituality

BELIEVE IN YOURSELF

HOW TO PROSPER

MEDITATIONS & AFFIRMATIONS

THE HEALING POWER OF
YOUR SUBCONSCIOUS MIND

Dr. Joseph Murphy

MEDIA

Published 2019 by Gildan Media LLC
aka G&D Media
www.GandDmedia.com

Front cover design by David Rheinhardt of Pyrographx

Interior design by Meghan Day Healey of Story Horse, LLC

Library of Congress Cataloging-in-Publication Data is available upon
request

ISBN: 978-1-7225-0279-9

10   9   8   7   6   5   4   3   2   1

CONTENTS

Believe
In Yourself

Believe
In Yourself

Dr. Joseph Murphy

CONTENTS

Chapter One
Make Your Dreams Come True

Joseph, in the Bible, means "disciplined or controlled imagination." It is one of the primal faculties of mind, and has the power to project and clothe your ideas, giving them visibility on the screen of space.

Israel loved Joseph. *Israel* is the spiritually awakened man who knows the power of controlled imagination. It is called the "son of his old age." *Son* means "expression." *Old age* infers wisdom and knowledge of the laws of mind. When you become familiar with the power of imagination, you will call it "the son of your old age." *Age* is not the flight of years; it is really the dawn of wisdom and Divine knowledge in you.

Imagination is the mighty instrument used by great scientists, artists, physicists, inventors, architects, and mystics. When the world said, "It is impossible; it can't be done," the man with imagination said, "It *is* done!" Through your imagination, you can also penetrate the depths of reality, and reveal the secrets of nature.

A great industrialist told me one time how he started in a small store. He said that I used to dream (Joseph was a dreamer) of a large corporation with branches all over the country. He added that regularly and systematically he pictured in his mind the giant building, offices, factories, and stores, knowing that through the alchemy of the mind, he could weave the fabric out of which his dreams would be clothed.

He prospered, and began to attract to himself—by a universal law of attraction—the ideas, personnel, friends, money, and everything needed for the unfoldment of his ideal. He truly exercised and cultivated his imagination, and lived with these mental patterns in his mind until imagination clothed them in form.

I particularly liked one comment that he made as follows: "It is just as easy to imagine yourself successful, as it is to imagine failure, and far more interesting."

Joseph is a dreamer, and a dreamer of dreams; this means he has visions, images, and ideals in his mind, and knows that there is a Creative Power that responds to his mental pictures. The mental images we hold are developed in feeling. It is wisely said that all our senses are modifications of the one-sense-feeling. Thomas Troward, a teacher of mental science, says, "Feeling is the law, and the law is the feeling." Feeling is the fountainhead of power. We must charge our mental pictures with feeling in order to get results.

We are told, "Joseph dreamed a dream, and told it to his brethren, and they hated him." Perhaps as you read this, you have a dream, an ideal, a plan, or purpose that you would like to accomplish. *To hate* is to reject in Bible language. The thoughts, feelings, beliefs, and opinions in your mind are the brethren that challenge you, belittle your dreams, and say to you, "You can't; it is impossible. Forget it!"

Perhaps other thoughts come into your mind that scoff at your plan or ambition. You discover that there is a quarrel in your mind with your own brethren; opposition sets in. The way to handle the opposition in your mind is to detach your attention from sense evidence and the appearance of things, and begin to think clearly and with interest about your goal or objective. When your mind is engaged on your goal or objective, you are using the creative law of mind, and it will come to pass.

"Lo, my sheaf arose, and also stood upright; and, behold, your sheaves stood round about, and made obeisance to my sheaf." Lift your ideal or desire up in consciousness. Exalt it. Commit yourself wholeheartedly to it. Praise it; give your attention, love, and devotion to your ideal; and as you continue to do so, all the fearful thoughts will make obeisance to your exalted state of mind—that is, they will lose their power and disappear from the mind.

Through your faculty to imagine the end result, you have control over any circumstance or condition. If you wish to bring about the realization of any wish, desire, or idea, form a mental picture of fulfillment in your mind; constantly imagine the reality of your desire. In this way, you will actually compel it into being. What you imagine as true already exists in the next dimension of mind, and if you remain faithful to your ideal, it will one day objectify itself. The master architect within you will project on the screen of visibility what you impress on your mind.

Joseph (imagination) wears a coat of many colors. A *coat* in the Bible is a psychological covering. Your psychological garments are the mental attitudes, moods, and feelings you entertain. *The coat of many colors* represent the many facets of the diamond, or your capacity to clothe any idea in form. You can imagine your friend who is poor living in the lap of luxury. You can see his face light up with joy, see his expression change, and a broad smile cross his lips. You can hear him tell you what you want to hear. You can see him exactly as you wish to see him—that is, he is radiant, happy, prosperous, and successful. Your imagination is the *coat of many colors;* it can clothe and objectify any idea or desire. You can imagine abundance where lack is, peace where discord is, and health where sickness is.

"His brethren said to him, 'Shalt thou indeed reign over us?'" Imagination is the first faculty, and takes precedence over all the other powers or elements of consciousness. You have 12 faculties or brethren, but your imagination when disciplined enables you to collapse time and space and rise above all limitations. When you keep your imagination busy with noble, Godlike concepts and ideas, you will find that it is the most effective of all faculties in your ongoing spiritual quest.

The phrase "Joseph is sold into Egypt" means that your concept or desire must be subjectified (Egypt) first before it becomes objectified. Every concept must go "down into Egypt," meaning into the subjective where the birth of ideas takes place.

"Out of Egypt have I called my son": Joseph is the commander of Egypt, which tells you that imagination controls the whole conceptive realm. Whatever prison you may be in, whether it is the prison of fear, sickness, lack, or limitation of any kind, remember that Joseph is the commander in prison and can deliver you. You can imagine your freedom, and continue to do so until it is subjectified; then, after gestation in the darkness, the manifestation comes—your prayer is answered.

Consider for a moment a distinguished, talented architect; he can build a beautiful, modern, 20th-century city in his mind, complete with super highways, swimming pools, aquariums, parks, and so on. He can construct in his mind the most beautiful palace the eye has ever seen. He can see the building in its entirety completely erected before he ever gives his plan to the builders. Where was the building? It was in his imagination.

With *your* imagination, you can actually hear the invisible voice of your mother even though she lives 10,000 miles from here. You can also see her clearly, and as vividly as if she were present; this is the wonderful power you possess. *You* can develop and cultivate this power, and become successful and prosperous.

Haven't you heard the sales manager say, "I have to let John go, because his attitude is wrong"? The business world knows the importance of "right attitude."

I remember many years ago having printed a small article on reincarnation. These pamphlets were on display on a book counter of a church where I lectured. In the beginning, very few of them were sold because the salesgirl was violently opposed to its contents.

I explained the Biblical meaning of reincarnation to her, the origin of the story, and what it was all about. She understood the contents of the drama, and became enthusiastic about the booklets; they were all sold before my lecture series was completed. This was an instance of the importance of the right mental attitude.

Your *mental attitude* means your mental reaction to people, circumstances, conditions, and objects in space. What is your relationship with your co-workers? Are you friendly with people, with animals, and with the universe in general? Do you think that the universe is hostile, and that the world owes you a living? In short, what is your attitude?

The emotional reaction of the above-mentioned girl was one of deep-seated prejudice. That was the *wrong attitude* in selling books; she was biased toward the book and the writer.

You can develop the right mental attitude when you realize that nothing externally can upset you or hurt you without your mental consent. You are the only thinker in your world; consequently, nothing can move you to anger, grief, or sorrow without your mental consent. The suggestions that come to you from the outside have no power whatsoever, except that you permit them to move you in thought negatively. Realize that you are master of your thought-world. Emotions follow thought; hence, you are supreme in your own orbit. Do you permit others to influence you? Do you allow the headlines in the newspapers, the gossip, or the criticism of others to upset you or bring about mental depression? If you do, you must admit you that are the cause of your own mood; you created your emotional reaction. Your attitude is wrong.

Do you imagine evil of others? If you do, notice the emotion generated in your deeper self; it is negative and destructive to your health and prosperity. Circumstances can affect you only as you permit them. You can voluntarily and definitely change your attitude toward life and all things. You can become master of your fate and captain of your soul (subconscious mind). Through disciplined, directed, and controlled imagination, you can dominate and master your emotions and mental attitude in general.

If you imagine, for example, that another person is mean, dishonest, and jealous, notice the emotion you evoked within yourself. Now reverse the situation. Begin to imagine the same person as honest, sincere, loving, and kind; notice the reaction it calls forth in you. Are you not, therefore, master of your attitudes?

In reality, the truth of the whole matter is that it is your real concept of God that determines your whole attitude toward life in general. Your dominant idea about God is your idea of life, for God is life. If you have the dominant idea or attitude that God is the Spiritual Power within you responsive to your thought, and that, therefore, since your habitual thinking is constructive and harmonious, this Power is guiding and prospering you in all ways, this dominant attitude will color everything. You will be looking at the world through the positive, affirmative attitude of mind. Your outlook will be positive, and you will have a joyous expectancy of the best.

Many people have a gloomy, despondent outlook on life. They are sour, cynical, and cantankerous; this is due to the dominant mental attitude that directs their reaction to everything.

A young boy of 16 years going to high school said to me, "I am getting very poor grades. My memory is failing. I do not know what's the matter." The only thing wrong was his attitude. He adopted a new mental attitude by realizing how important his studies were in gaining entrance grades to college in order to become a lawyer. He began to pray scientifically, which is one of the quickest ways to change the mentality.

In scientific prayer, we deal with a principle that responds to thought. This young man realized that there was a Spiritual Power within him, and that It was the only Cause and Power. Furthermore, he began to claim that his memory was perfect, and that Infinite

Intelligence constantly revealed to him everything he needed to know at all times, everywhere. He began to radiate love and goodwill to the teachers and fellow students. This young man is now enjoying a greater freedom than he had known for several years. He constantly imagines the teachers and his mother congratulating him on all A's. It is imagining the desired results that have followed this change of attitude toward his studies.

We have said previously that all our mental attitudes are conditioned by imagination. If you imagine that it is going to be a black day today, that business is going to be very poor, that it is raining, that no customers will come into your store, that they have no money, and so on, you will experience the result of your negative imagery.

One time a man was walking the streets of London, and he imagined he saw a snake on the street. Fear caused him to become semi-paralyzed. What he saw *looked* like a snake, but he had the same mental and emotional reaction as if it were a snake.

Imagine whatsoever things are lovely, noble, and of good report, and your entire emotional attitude toward life will change. What do you imagine about life? Is it going to be a happy life for you? Or is it one long series of frustrations? "Choose ye whom ye will serve."

You mold, fashion, and shape your outer world of experience according to the mental images you habitually dwell on. Imagine conditions and circumstances in life that dignify, elevate, please, and satisfy. If you imagine that life is cold, cruel, hard, bitter, and that struggle and pain are inevitable, you are making life miserable for yourself.

Imagine yourself on the golf course. You are free, relaxed, and full of enthusiasm and energy. Your joy is in overcoming all the difficulties presented by the golf course. The thrill is in surmounting all the obstacles.

Now let us take this scene: Imagine yourself going into a funeral parlor. Notice the different emotional response brought forward as you picture yourself in each of the above-mentioned situations. In the funeral chapel, you can rejoice in the person's new birthday. You can imagine the loved one surrounded by his or her friends in the midst of indescribable beauty and love. You can imagine God's river of peace flooding the minds and hearts of all present. You can actually ascend the heavens of your own mind wherever you are; this is the power of your imagination.

"And he dreamed yet another dream, and told it his brethren, and said, 'Behold, I have dreamed a dream more; and behold, the sun and the moon and the eleven stars made obeisance to me.'"

In ancient symbology, the sun and the moon represent the conscious and subconscious mind. The 11 stars represent the 11 powers in addition to imagination. Here again, the inspired writers are telling you that disciplined imagination takes precedence over all other faculties of the mind, and controls the direction of the conscious and subconscious mind. Imagination is first and foremost; it can be scientifically directed.

I was examining one of the Round Towers of Ireland with my father over 50 years ago. He said nothing for one hour, but remained passive and receptive, seeming to be in a pensive mood. I asked him what he was meditating on. This is the essence of his answer: He pointed out that it is only by dwelling on the great, wonderful ideas of the world that we grow and expand. He contemplated the age of the stones in the tower, then his imagination took him back to the quarries where stones were first formed. His imagination unclothed the stones. He saw with the interior eye the structure, the geological formation, the composition of the stone, and reduced it to the formless state; finally, he imagined the oneness of the stones with all stones and with all life. He realized in his Divine imagery that it was possible to reconstruct the history of the Irish race from looking at the Round Tower!

Through the imaginative faculty, this teacher was able to see the invisible men living in the Tower and to hear their voices. The whole place became alive to him in his imagination. Through this power, he was able to go back in time when there was no Round Tower there. In his mind, he began to weave a drama of the place from which stones originated, who brought them, the purpose of the structure, and the history connected with it. As he said to me, "I am able to almost feel the touch, and hear the sound, of steps that vanished thousands of years ago."

The subjective mind permeates all things; it is in all things, and is the substance from which they are made. The treasure house of eternity is in the very stones comprising a building. There is nothing inanimate; all is life in its varied manifestations. (The sun and the moon make obeisance to Joseph—imagination.) Truly through your faculty of imagination you can imagine that the invisible secrets of nature are revealed to you; you will find that you can plumb the very depths of consciousness, calling things that be not as though they were, and the unseen becomes seen.

The other night I sat in a park, and looked at the setting sun. Suddenly I began to think that the sun is like a house in the city of Los Angeles; there is a greater sun behind our sun, and so on to infinity. It staggers the imagination to ponder and meditate on the myriads of suns and solar galaxies extending into infinity beyond the milky way. This world is only a grain of sand in the infinite seashore. Instead of seeing the parts, let us look at the wholeness, the unity of all things. We are, as the poet said, "All parts of one stupendous whole, whose body nature is, and God the soul."

It is really out of the imaginative mind of man that all religions are born. Is it not out of the realm of imagination that television, radio, radar, super jets, and all other modern inventions came? Your imagination is the treasure house of infinity, which releases to you all the precious jewels of music, art, poetry, and inventions. You can look at some ancient ruin, an old temple, or pyramid, and reconstruct the records of the dead past. In the ruins of an old church yard, you can also see a modern city resurrected in all its beauty and glory. You may be in a prison of want, lack, or behind stone bars, but in your imagination you can find an undreamed of measure of freedom.

Remember how Chico, the Parisian sewer cleaner, imagined and lived in a paradisaical state of mind called the seventh heaven even though he never saw the light of day?

Bunyan, in prison, wrote the great masterpiece *Pilgrim's Progress*. Milton, although blind, saw with the interior eye. His imagination made his brain a ball of fire, and he wrote *Paradise Lost*. In this way he brought some of God's paradise to all people everywhere.

Imagination was Milton's spiritual eye, which enabled him to go about God's business whereby he annihilated time, space, and matter, and brought forth the truths of the Invisible Presence and Power.

A genius is a man who is in rapport with his subconscious mind. He is able to tap this universal reservoir and receive answers to his problems; thus, he does not have to work by the sweat of his brow. In the genius type of mind, the imaginative faculty is developed to a very high degree. All great poets and writers are gifted with a highly developed and cultivated imaginative faculty.

I can now see Shakespeare listening to the old stories, fables, and myths of his day. I can also imagine him sitting down listing all these characters in the play in his mind . . . then clothing them one by one with hair, skin, muscle, and bone; animating them; and making them so much alive that we think we are reading about ourselves.

Use your imagination and go about your Father's business. *Your Father's business* is to let your wisdom, skill, knowledge, and ability come forth, and bless others as well as yourself. You are about your Father's business if you are operating a small store, and in your imagination you feel you are operating a larger store giving a greater measure of service to your fellow creature.

If you are a writer of short stories, you can be about your Father's business. Create a story in your mind that teaches something about the golden rule, then pass that story and all its characters through your spiritualized and highly artistic mentality; your article will be fascinating and intensely interesting to your public.

The truth about man is always wonderful and beautiful. When writing a novel or story, we should be sure that we clothe Truth in her garment of loveliness and beauty. You could now look at an acorn, and with your imaginative eye construct a magnificent forest full of rivers, rivulets, and streams. You could people the forest with all kinds of life; furthermore, you could hang a bow on every cloud. You could look at a desert, and cause it to rejoice and blossom as a rose. "Instead of the thorn shall come up the fir tree, and instead of the briar shall come up the myrtle tree." Men gifted with intuition and imagination find water in the desert, and they create cities where formerly other men only saw a desert and a wilderness.

An architect of a city sees the buildings and fountains already in operation before he ever digs a well or builds a house. "I will make the wilderness a pool of water, and the dry land springs of water."

Long hours, hard labor, or burning the midnight oil will not produce a Milton, a Shakespeare, or a

Beethoven. People accomplish great things through quiet moments, imagining that the invisible things from the foundation of time are clearly visible.

You can imagine the indescribable beauty of He Who Is being expressed on your canvas, and if you are a real artist in love with beauty, great beauty will come forth effortlessly. Moments of great inspiration will come to you; it will have nothing to do with perspiration or hard, mental labor.

In Greenwich Village, I met a poet who wrote beautiful poems; he had them printed on cards, and sold them at Christmastime. Some of these poems were beautiful gems of spiritual love. He said that when he got still, the words would come into his mind accompanied by a lovely scene. Flowers, people, and friends would come clearly into his mind. These images spoke to him. They told him their story. Oftentimes the entire poem, song, or lullaby would appear complete and ready in his mind without the slightest effort. His habit was to imagine that he was writing beautiful poems that would stir the hearts of men.

Shelley said that poetry was an expression of the imagination. When the poet meditates on love, and wishes to write on love, the Invisible Intelligence and Wisdom within him stirs his mind, casts the spell of God's beauty over him, and awakens him to God's

Eternal Love so that his words become clothed with wisdom, truth, and beauty.

The Great Musician is within. If it is your business to play music or compose music, be sure that you are on your Father's Business. Your *Father's Business* is first of all to recognize God as the Great Musician; then meditate, feel, pray, and know that the Inner Music sings or plays through you the Song of God's Love, and you will play like you have never played before.

Every invention of Edison's was first conceived in his imagination. The same was true of Tesla, another great inventor and scientist.

I think it was Oliver Wendell Holmes who said that we need three story men who can idealize, imagine, and predict. I believe it was the capacity to imagine and dream that caused Ford to look forward to putting the world on wheels.

Your capacity to imagine causes you, and enables you, to remove all barriers of time and space. You can reconstruct the past or contemplate the future thought through your inner eye. No wonder it says in Genesis: "Israel loved Joseph [imagination] more than all his brethren." Imagination, when disciplined, spiritualized, controlled, and directed becomes the most exalted and noblest attribute of man.

I was in a conversation some years ago with a young chemist who stated that his superiors for years had tried to manufacture a certain German dye and failed. He was given the assignment when he went with them. As he commented, he did not know that it could not be done, and synthesized the compound without any difficulty. They were amazed and wanted to know his secret. His answer was that he imagined he had the answer. Pressed further by his superiors, he said that he could clearly see the letters "Answer!" in blazing red color in his mind; then he created a vacuum underneath the letters, knowing that as he imagined the chemical formula underneath the letters, the subconscious would fill it in. The third night he had a dream in which the complete formula and the technique of making the compound was clearly presented.

"Joseph [imagination] is a dreamer, and a dreamer of dreams." "They conspired against him to slay him. And they said one to another, Behold, this dreamer cometh." Perhaps as you read these Biblical quotations there are thoughts of fear, doubt, and anxiety conspiring in your own mind to slay or kill that desire, ideal, or dream of yours. You look at conditions or circumstances, and fear arises in your mind; yet there is the desire within you which, if realized, would bring you peace and solve your problem.

You must be like Joseph and become a practical dreamer. Decide to make your dreams come true. Withdraw, and abstract your attention now from appearances of things and from sense evidence. Even though your senses deny what you pray for, affirm that it is true in your heart. Bring your mind back from its wandering after the false Gods of fear and doubt, to rest in the Omnipotence of the Spiritual Power within you. In the silence and quietude of your own mind, dwell on the fact that there is only One Power and One Presence. This Power and Presence is now responding to your thought as guidance, strength, peace, and nourishment for the soul. Give all your mental attention to recognizing the absolute sovereignty of the Spiritual Power, knowing that the God-Power has the answer and is now showing you the way. Trust It, believe in It, and walk the earth in the Light your prayer is already answered.

All of us read the story of Columbus and his discovery of America. It was imagination that led him to his discovery. His imagination plus faith in a Divine Power led him on and brought him to victory.

The sailors said to Columbus, "What shall we do when all hope is gone?" His reply was, "You shall say at break of day, 'Sail on, sail on, and on.'" Here is the key to prayer; be faithful to the end; full of faith every step of the way, persisting to the end, knowing in your heart that the end is secure because you saw the end.

Copernicus through his vivid imagination revealed how the earth revolved on its axis, causing the old astronomical theories to be cast in the discard.

I think it would be a wonderful idea if all of us from time to time recast our ideas, checked up on our beliefs and opinions, and asked ourselves honestly, "Why do I believe that? Where did that opinion come from?" Perhaps many ideas, theories, beliefs, and opinions that we hold are completely erroneous, and were accepted by us as true without any investigation whatever as to their truth or accuracy. Because our father and grandfather believed in a certain way is no reason why we should.

One woman said to me that a certain idea she had must be true because her grandmother believed it. That is absurd! The race mind believes in many things that aren't true. What came down from generation to generation is not necessarily valid, or the final word and authority.

The above-mentioned woman who was honest and well-meaning had a mind that was very touchy on psychological truths. She took everything in the Bible literally. This mind worked by prejudice, superstition, and opposed everything that was not in accord with her established beliefs, opinions, and preconceived notions.

Our mind must be like a parachute. The latter opens up; if it does not, it isn't any good. Likewise, we must open our eyes and minds to new truths. We must hunger and thirst after new truth and new knowledge, enabling us to soar aloft above our problems on the wings of faith and understanding.

The famous biologists, physicists, astronomers, and mathematicians of our day are men gifted with a vivid, scientific imagination. For instance, the Einstein theory of relativity existed first in his imagination.

Archeologists and paleontologists studying the tombs of ancient Egypt through their imaginative perception reconstruct ancient scenes. The dead past becomes alive and audible once more. Looking at the ancient ruins and the hieroglyphics thereon, the scientist tells us of an age when there was no language. Communication was done by grunts, groans, and signs. The scientist's imagination enables him to clothe this ancient temple with roofs; and surround them with gardens, pools, and fountains. The fossil remains are clothed with eyes, sinews, and muscles, and they again walk and talk. The past becomes the living present, and we find in imagination that there is no time or space. Through your imaginative faculty, you can be a companion of the most inspired writers of all time.

I gave a lecture on the 21st chapter of Revelation sometime ago in the Wilshire Ebell Theater in Los Angeles to our Sunday audience. The previous night while I was meditating on the inner meaning of the following verses, I intuitively and actually felt the presence and the intimate companionship of the mystic seer who wrote the inspired verses.

"And I John saw the holy city, new Jerusalem, coming down from God out of heaven, prepared as a bride adorned for her husband. And I heard a great voice out of heaven saying, Behold, the tabernacle of God is with men, and he will dwell with them, and be their God." (Rev. 21:2, 2)

Can't you now walk down the corridor of your own mind, and there see, inwardly perceive, feel, and sense God's river of peace flowing through your mind? You are now in the Holy City—your own mind—inhabited by such lovely people as bliss, joy, faith, harmony, love, and goodwill. Your mind is clothed with God's radiant beauty; and your mood is exalted, noble, and Godlike. You are married mentally and spiritually to God and to all things good. You have on your wedding garment, because you are in tune with the Infinite, and God's Eternal Verities constantly impregnate your mind. In your imagination, you sense and feel that you are the tabernacle of God, and that His Holy Spirit saturates and fills every part of your being. Your imagination now becomes seized with a Divine frenzy. You become God-intoxicated, having received the Divine antibody, the Presence of God in the chamber of your heart.

You can look at a rock, and out of that rock through Divine Imagination you can reveal the Madonna, and portray a vision of beauty and a joy forever. Never permit your imagination to be used negatively; never distort or twist it. You can imagine sickness, accident, and loss and become a mental wreck. To imagine sickness and lack is to destroy your peace of mind, health, and happiness.

On board ship one time I heard a passenger exclaim when looking at the setting sun, "I am so happy, I hope this lasts forever!"

How often have you seen a glorious sunrise—perhaps you said, "I hope this lasts forever?" Nothing in this transitory world lasts eternally; however, the Truths of God last forever. Darkness follows night, but morning will come again. Twilight will also come. You do not want things to stand still. You do not want to stand still either, for there are new worlds within and without to conquer. Change eternal is at the root of all life.

You do not want to remain in a rut. Problems are life's way of asking you for an answer. The greatest joy and satisfaction is in overcoming, in conquering. Life would become unbearable and unendurable if we did not experience change. We would be bored by the monotony of things. You meet with night and day, cold and heat, ebb and flow, summer and winter, hope and despair, success and failure. You find yourself moving through opposites; through your power to imagine what you wish and to feel its reality subjectively is to reconcile the opposites and bring peace to the mind.

In the midst of sorrow, grief, or the loss of a loved one, your imagination and faith—the two wings of the bird—take you aloft into the very Bosom of God, your Father, where you find peace, solace, and Divine rest for your soul.

In your imagination, you look into the very Face or Truth of God; and God wipes away all tears, and there shall be no more crying. All the mist and fog of the human mind dissolves in the sunshine of God's Love.

"And God shall wipe away all tears from their eyes; and there shall be no more death, neither sorrow, nor crying; neither, shall there be any more pain: for the former things are passed away. Behold I make all things new." (Rev. 4, 5.)

When the night is black, you see no way out; that is, when your problem is most acute, let your imagination be your savior.

"I will lift up mine eyes [imagination] unto the hills, from whence cometh my help." (Ps. 121: 1.) *The hills* are of an inner range—the Presence of God in you. When you seek guidance and inspiration, fix your eyes on the stars of God's Truth, such as "Infinite Intelligence leads and guides me," or "Divine Wisdom floods my mind, and I am inspired from on High."

There is a designer, an architect, and a weaver within you; it takes the fabric of your mind, your thoughts, feelings, and beliefs; and molds them into a pattern of life that brings you peace or discord, health or sickness. You can imagine a life that will take you up to the third heaven, where you will see unspeakable and unutterable things of God; or through the distorted, morbid use of your imagination you can sink to the depths of degradation.

Man is the tabernacle of God, and no matter how low a man has sunk, the Healing Presence is there waiting to minister to him. It is within us waiting for us to call upon It. You can use your imagination in all business transactions in a wonderful way. Always imagine yourself in the other fellow's place; this tells you what to do. Imagine that the other is expressing all that you long to see him express. See him as he ought to be, not as he appears to be. Perhaps he is surly, sarcastic, bitter, or hostile; there may be many frustrated hopes and tragedies lurking in his mind. Imagine whatsoever things are lovely and of good report, and through your imagination you have covered him with the garment of God. God's world of ideals and God's infinite ideas are within him, waiting to be born and released. You can say if you wish, "God waits to be born in him." You can open the door, and kindle the fire of God's Love in that man's heart, and perhaps the spark you lit will burst into a Divine Fire.

The greatest and richest galleries of art in the world are the galleries of the mind devoted to God's Truths and Beauty. Leonardo Da Vinci, through his gift of imagination, meditated on Jesus and the Twelve Disciples, and what they meant. Lost in deep reverie, his imagination secreted the perfect pictures from the Infinite Reservoir within him, and due to his perfect focus his inner eye glowed with an interior luminosity, so that he was inspired, and out of his Divine Imagery came the masterpiece: "The Last Supper."

You have visited a quiet lake or a mountaintop. Notice how the placid, cool, calm surface reflected the heavenly lights, so does the quiet mind of the spiritual man reflect God's interior Lights and Wisdom.

Picture your ideal in life; live with this ideal. Let the ideal captivate your imagination; let the ideal thrill you! You will move in the direction of the ideal that governs your mind. The ideals of life are like the dew of heaven that move over the arid areas of man's mind, refreshing and invigorating him.

The inspired writer's imagination was fired with Truth when he wrote: "There is a river the streams whereof shall make glad the city of God, the holy place of the tabernacles of the most High." (Ps. 46:4.)

By now you know that imagination is the river enabling *you* to flow back psychologically to God. The streams and rivulets are your ideas and feelings, plus the emanation of love and goodwill that goes forth from you to all men everywhere. Man looks out into the world; and he sees sickness, chaos, and man's inhumanity to man. The man with the disciplined imagination soars above all appearances, discord, sense evidence, and sees the sublime principle of harmony operating through, in, and behind all things. He knows through his Divine imagery that there is an Everlasting Law of Righteousness behind all things, an Ever-Abiding Peace, a Boundless Love governing the entire Cosmos. These Truths surge through the heart, and are born of the eternal Truth which through the imagination pierces the outer veil, and rests in the Divine meaning of the way it is in God and Heaven.

Imagination was the workshop of God that inspired the writer of the following matchless, spiritual gems—which will go down through the corridor of time and live forever. For tender beauty and for Divine imagery, they are unsurpassed in dealing with the availability and Immanence of God's Presence:

"For he shall give his angels charge over thee, to keep thee in all thy ways." (Ps. 91: 11.)

"Whither shall I go from thy spirit? or whither shall I flee from thy presence?"

"If I ascend up into heaven, thou art there if I make my bed in hell, behold, thou *art there.*"

"If I take the wings of the morning, and dwell in the uttermost parts of the sea; even there shall thy hand lead me, and thy right hand shall hold me."

CHAPTER TWO

Using the Subconscious Mind in Business

Long before our Bible was published, ancient wisdom said, "As a man imagines and feels, so does he become." This ancient teaching is lost in the night of time; it is lost in antiquity.

The Bible states, "As a man thinketh in his heart, so is he."

Legend relates that many thousands of years ago the Chinese sages gathered together under the leadership of a great sage to discuss the fact that vast legends of brutal invaders were pillaging and plundering the land. The question to be resolved was: "How shall we preserve the ancient wisdom from the destruction of the invaders?"

There were many suggestions: Some thought that the ancient scrolls and symbols should be buried in the Himalayan mountains. Others suggested that the wisdom be deposited in monasteries in Tibet. Still others pointed out that the sacred temples of India were the ideal places for the preservation of the wisdom of their God.

The chief sage was silent during the entire discussion; in fact, he went to sleep in the midst of their talk and snored loudly, much to their dismay! He awakened in a little while, and said, "Tao [God] gave me the answer, and it is this: 'We will order the great pictorial artists of China—men gifted with Divine imagination—[which is the workshop of God] and tell them what we wish to accomplish. We will initiate them into the mysteries of Truth. They will portray or depict in picture form, the great Truths which shall be preserved for all time, and for countless generations yet unborn. When they are finished with the dramatization of the great Truths, Powers, Qualities, and Attributes of God through a series of picture cards, we will tell the world about a new game that has been originated. Men throughout the world for all time will use them as a game of chance, not knowing that through this simple device, they are preserving the sacred teaching for all generations.'" This was the origin of our own deck of cards.

The ancient Chinese sage, according to the legend, added, "If all the sacred writings were destroyed, they could again be resurrected at any time through the symbolic teachings and inner meanings of the various designs on the playing cards."

Imagination clothes all ideas and gives them form. Through the Divine artistry of imagination, these artists clothed all these ideas with pictorial form. In the act of imagination, that which is hidden in your deeper self is made manifest. Through imagination, what exists in latency or is asleep within you is given form in thought. We contemplate that which hitherto had been unrevealed.

Let us take some simple examples: When you were going to be married, you had vivid, realistic pictures in your mind. With your power of imagination, you saw the minister, rabbi, or priest. You heard him pronounce the words; you saw the flowers, the church, and you heard the music. You imagined the ring on your finger, and you traveled through your imagination on your honeymoon to Niagara Falls or Europe. All this was performed by your imagination.

Likewise before graduation, you had a beautiful, scenic drama taking place in your mind; you had clothed all your ideas about graduation in form. You imagined the professor or the president of the college giving you your diploma. You saw all the students dressed in gowns. You heard your mother or father or your girl- or boyfriend congratulate you. You felt the embrace and the kiss; it was all real, dramatic, exciting, and wonderful. Images appeared freely in your mind as if from nowhere, but you know and must admit that there was and is an Internal Creator with Power to mold all these forms that you saw in your mind; and endow them with life, motion, and voice. These images said to you, "For you only we live!"

A young man said to me in the army before he was discharged, "I see my mother clearly. I can now imagine her welcome. I see the old home. Father is smoking a pipe. My sister is feeding the dogs. I can see every mark and corner of that home. I can even hear their voices."

Where do all these vivid pictures come from? Keats said that there is an ancestral wisdom in man, and we can, if we wish, drink of that old wine of heaven.

The spirit or God in you is the real basis of imagination. Once in an examination in London, I did not know the answer to an important question. I got still and quiet, and said over and over again slowly, meditating in a relaxed way, "God reveals the answer!" In the meantime, I went on answering the other questions, which were easy.

We know that when you relax the conscious mind, the subjective wisdom rises to the fore. In a short while, the picture of the answer came clearly into my mind. It was there in words like a page of a book, with the entire answer written out as a graph in the mind. A Mightier Wisdom than that of my conscious mind or intellect spoke through me.

I had a very religious school boy about 14 years old come to me. Whenever he had a problem, he said to me that he would imagine Jesus was talking to him, giving him the answer to his problem, and telling him what to do. His mother was very ill; this boy was highly imaginative. He read the story of Jesus healing the woman with fever. My little friend related to me, "Last night I imagined Jesus saying to me, 'Go thy way; thy mother is made whole!'" He made that drama of the mind so real, vivid, and intense, that due to his faith and belief, he convinced himself of the truth of what he heard subjectively.

His mother was completely healed, yet she was considered at that time hopeless and beyond medical help.

Being a student of the laws of mind, you know what happened. He galvanized himself into the feeling of being one with his image, and according to his faith or conviction was it done unto him. There is only One Mind and One Healing Presence. As the boy changed his conviction about his mother and felt her perfect health, the idea of perfect health was resurrected in her mind simultaneously. He did not know anything about spiritual healing or the power of imagination. He operated the law unconsciously, and believed in his own mind that Jesus was actually talking to him; then, according to his belief, was it done unto him.

To believe something is to accept it as true. This is why Paracelsus said in the 16th century, "Whether the object of your belief be true or false, you will get the same results." There is only one spiritual, healing Principle and one Process of healing called *faith*. "According to your faith is it done unto you." There are many processes, methods, and techniques of healing, and all of them get results—not because of the particular technique or method, but because of imagination and faith in the particular process. They are all tapping the One Source of healing, which is God. The Infinite Healing Presence permeates all things and is omnipresent.

The voodoo doctor with his incantations gets results. So does the kahuna of Hawaii with his ministrations, the various branches of New Thought and Christian Science, the Nancy School of Medicine, osteopathy, and so on. All these schools of thought are meeting levels of consciousness and are doing good.

Any method or process that alleviates human misery, pain, and distress is good. Many churches practice the laying on of hands; others make novenas and visit shrines; all are benefited according to their mental acceptance or belief.

When you are willing to stand alone with God and cease completely giving power to external things, when you no longer give power to the phenomenalistic world, which means to make a world of effect a cause; when all your allegiance is given to the Spiritual Power within you, realizing it as the only Presence and the only Cause, you will not need any props of any kind. The Living Intelligence that made your body will respond immediately to your faith and understanding; and you will have an instantaneous, spiritual healing. If you are not at that level of consciousness where you can grow a tooth through prayer, the obvious thing to do is to go see a dentist. Pray for him and for a perfect, Divine, oral adjustment. As long as you believe in external causes, you will seek external remedies.

To illustrate further the power of imagination, I will tell you about a close relative of mine who had tuberculosis. His lungs were badly diseased, so his son decided to heal his father. He came home to Perth, Western Australia, where his father lived, and said to him that he had met a monk who sold him a piece of

the true cross, and that he gave him the equivalent of
$500 for it. (This young man had picked up a splinter
of wood off the sidewalk, went to a jeweler's, and had
it set in a ring so that it looked real.) He told his father
that many were healed just by touching the ring or the
cross. He inflamed and fired his father's imagination
to the point that the old gentleman snatched the ring
from him, placed it over his chest, prayed silently, and
went to sleep. In the morning, he was healed; all the
clinic's tests were negative.

You know, of course, that it was not the splinter
of wood from the sidewalk that healed him. It was
his imagination aroused to an intense degree, plus
the confident expectancy of a perfect healing. Imagination was joined to faith or subjective feeling, and
the union of the two brought about the healing. The
father never learned the trick that had been played
upon him; if he had, he probably would have had a
relapse. He remained completely cured, and passed
away 15 years later at the age of 89.

I know a businessman here in Los Angeles who
has reached the top in his field. He told me that for
30 years the most important decisions he ever made
were based on his imaginary conversations with Paul.
I asked him to elaborate, and he remarked that few
people in the business world realized the wonderful
guidance and counsel they could receive by drama-

tizing in their imagination that they were receiving counsel from the writers or great seers of the Bible.

I will quote this successful executive as accurately as I can: "Many times my decisions might have prospered the company or plunged it into bankruptcy. I vacillated, wavered, got high blood pressure, and heart disease. One day the idea came to me: Why not ask Jesus or Paul? I loved the Epistles of Paul, so when an important decision was to be made, I would imagine Paul was saying to me: 'Your decision is perfect; it will bless your organization. Bless you, my son! Keep on God's path.' After imagining I saw Paul and heard him, a wave of peace and inner tranquillity would seize me; I was at peace about all decisions."

This was this businessman's way of receiving Divine Guidance by using his imagination to convince himself that right action was his. There is only one Principle of Intelligence in this world; all that is really necessary is to say and believe, "God is guiding me now, and there is only right action in my life."

The mind, as Troward tells you, works like a syllogism. If your premise is correct, the conclusion or result will correspond. The subjective reasons deductively only, and its sequence or conclusion is always in harmony with the premise. Establish the right premise in your mind; you will be subjectively compelled to right action. Inner movement of the mind is action.

The external movements and action is the automatic response of the body to the internal motion of the mind. Hearing a friend or associate congratulate you on your wonderful decision will induce the movement of right action in your life.

The man who used St. Paul to impregnate his mind with the belief of right action was using the One Eternal Principle of Intelligence. His technique of arriving at that place in his mind does not really matter.

Goethe used his imagination wisely when confronted with difficulties and predicaments. His biographers point out that he was accustomed to filling many hours quietly holding imaginary conversations. It is well known that his custom was to imagine one of his friends before him in a chair answering in the right way. In other words, if he were concerned over any problems, he imagined that his friend was giving him the right or appropriate answer, accompanied with the usual gestures and tonal qualities of the voice, making the entire imaginary scene as real and vivid as possible.

I was very well acquainted with a stockbroker in New York City who used to attend my classes at Steinway Hall there. His method of solving financial difficulties was very simple. He would have mental, imaginary conversations with a multimillionaire banker-friend of his who used to congratulate him on his wise and sound judgment, and compliment him on his purchase of the right stocks. He used to dramatize this imaginary conversation until he had psychologically fixed it as a form of belief in his mind.

Mr. Nicols, Ouspensky's student, used to say, "Watch your inner talking, and let it agree with your aim."

This broker's inner talking or speech certainly agreed with his aim to make sound investments for himself and his clients. He told me that his main purpose in his business life was to make money for others, and to see them prosper financially by his wise counsel. It is quite obvious that he was using the laws of mind constructively.

Prayer is a habit. This broker regularly and at frequent intervals during the day returned to the mental image in his mind; he made it a deep, subjective pattern. That which is embodied subjectively is objectively expressed. It is the *sustained* mental picture that is developed in the dark house of the mind. Run your mental movie often. Get into the habit of flashing it on the screen of your mind frequently. After a while it will become a definite, habitual pattern. The inner movie that you have seen with your mind's eye shall be made manifest openly: "He calleth things that be not as though they were, and the unseen becomes seen."

Many people solve their dilemmas and problems by the play of their imagination, knowing that whatever they imagine and feel as true, will and must come to pass.

Sometime ago, a certain young woman was involved in a complicated lawsuit that had persisted for five years. There was one postponement after another, with no solution in sight. At my suggestion, she began to dramatize as vividly as possible her lawyer having an animated discussion with her regarding the outcome. She would ask him questions, and he would answer her appropriately; then she condensed the whole thing down to a simple phrase, as suggested years ago by the French School of Mental Therapeutics. She had him repeat it over and over again to her. The phrase she said was: "There has been a perfect, harmonious solution. The whole case is settled outside court."

She kept looking at the mental picture whenever she had a spare moment. While in a restaurant for a cup of coffee, she ran the mental movie with gestures, voice, and sound equipment. She could imagine easily the sound of his voice, smile, and mannerisms. She ran the movie so often that it became a subjective pattern—a regular train track. It was written in her mind; or as the Bible says, it was "written in her heart and inscribed in her inward parts." Her conclusion was: "It is God in action," meaning all-around harmony and peace. (*Harmony* is of God, and what you want in a legal case is a harmonious solution.)

In the science of imagination, you must first of all begin to discipline your imagination and not let it run riot. *Science* insists upon purity. If you wish a chemically pure product, you must remove all traces of other substances as well as extraneous material. You must, in other words, separate out and cast away all the dross.

In the science of imagination, you eliminate all the mental impurities, such as fear, worry, destructive inner talking, self-condemnation, and the mental union with other miscellaneous negatives. You must focus all your attention on your ideal, and refuse to be swerved from your purpose or aim in life. As you get mentally absorbed in the reality of your ideal, by loving and remaining faithful to it, you will see your desire take form in your world. In the book of Joshua it says, "Choose ye this day whom ye shall serve." Let your choice be, "I am going to imagine whatsoever things are lovely and of good report."

I know and have talked to many people who diabolically invert the use of their God-given faculty. The mother, for example, imagines that something bad has happened to her son, John, because he is late coming home. She imagines an accident, a hospital, Johnny in the operating room, and so on.

A businessman whose affairs are prospering, yet dwells on negativity, is another example of the destructive use of imagination. He comes home from the office, runs a motion picture in his mind of failure, sees the shelves empty, imagines himself going into bankruptcy, an empty bank balance, and the business closed down . . . yet all the time he is actually prospering. There is no truth whatsoever in that negative mental picture of his; it is a lie made out of whole cloth. In other words, the thing he fears does not exist save in his morbid imagination; the failure will never come to pass, except he keeps up that morbid picture charged with the emotion of fear. If he constantly indulges in this mental picture, he will, of course, bring failure to pass. He had the choice of failure or success, but he chose failure.

There are chronic worriers; they never seem to imagine anything good or lovely. They seem to know that something bad or destructive is always going to happen. They cannot tell you one reason why something good should and could happen; however, they are ready with all the reasons why something dire and evil should occur.

Why is this? The reason is simple: These people are habitually negative; that is, most of their thinking is of a negative, chaotic, destructive, morbid nature. As they continue to make a habit of these negative patterns of thought, they condition their subconscious mind negatively. Their imagination is governed by their dominant moods and feelings; this is why they imagine evil, even about their loved ones.

For example, if their son happens to be in the army, they imagine that he is going to catch cold, become an alcoholic, become loose morally; or if he is in combat, they imagine he will be shot, and all manner of destructive images enter their mind. This is due to the hypnotic spell of habit, and their prayers are rendered null and void.

Make a choice now! Begin to think constructively and harmoniously. *To think* is to speak. Your thought is your word. Let your words be as a honeycomb, sweet to the ear, and pleasant to the bones. Let your words be "like apples of Gold in pictures of silver." The future is the present grown up; it is your invisible word or thought made visible. Are your words sweet to the ear? What is your inner speech like at this moment? No one hear you; it is your own silent thought. Perhaps you are saying to yourself, "I can't; it is impossible." "I'm too old now." "What chance have I?" "Mary can, but I can't. I have no money. I can't afford this or that. I've tried; it's no use." You can see your words are not as a honeycomb; they are not sweet to your ear; they do not lift you up or inspire you.

Ouspensky was always stressing the importance of inner speech, inner conversation, or inner talking. It is really the way you feel inside; for the inside mirrors the outside. Is your inner speech pleasant to the bones? Does it exalt you, thrill you, and make you happy?

Bones are symbolic of support and symmetry. Let your inner talking sustain and strengthen you. "But the word is very nigh unto thee, in thy mouth, and in thy heart, that thou mayest do it. See, I have set before thee this day life and good, and death and evil."

Decree now, and say it meaningly: "From this moment forward, I will admit to my mind for mental consumption only those ideas and thoughts that heal, bless, inspire, and strengthen me." Let your words from now on be as "apples of gold in pictures of silver." An apple is a delicious fruit. *Gold* means "power." *Pictures of silver* mean in the Bible "your desires." The *picture* in your mind is the way you want things to be. It is the picture of your fulfilled desire. It could be a new position or health. Let your words, your inner silent thought, and feeling coincide and agree with the *Picture of silver* or your desire. Desire and feeling joined together in a mental marriage will become the answered prayer.

Be sure you follow the imagination of the Bible, and let your words be sweet to the ear. What are you giving *your ear* to now? What are you listening to? What are you giving attention to? Whatever you give attention to will grow, magnify, and multiply in your experience.

"Faith cometh by hearing," Paul says. Listen to the great truths of God. Listen to the voice of God. What language does He speak in? It is not Gaelic, French, or Italian; but the universal language or mood of love, peace, joy, harmony, faith, confidence, and goodwill. Give your ear to these qualities and potencies of God. Mentally eat of these qualities; and as you continue to do so, you will be conditioned to those positive, enduring qualities, and the Law of Love will govern you.

You have heard this oft-repeated quotation, "Man is made in the image and likeness of God." This means that your mind is God's mind, as there is only One Mind. Your Spirit is God's Spirit, and you create in exactly the same way, and through the same law as God creates. Your individual world; that is, experiences, conditions, circumstances, environment, as well as your physical health, financial states, and social life, et cetera., is made out of your own mental images and after your own likeness.

Like attracts like. Your world is a mirror reflecting back to you your inner world of thought, feeling, beliefs, and inner conversation. If you begin to imagine evil powers working against you, or that there is a jinx following you, or that other forces and people are working against you, there will be a response of your deeper mind to correspond with these negative pictures and fears in your mind; therefore, you will begin to say that everything is against you, or that the stars are opposed to you; or you will blame karma, your past lives, or some demon.

Truly the only sin is ignorance. Pain is not a punishment; it is the consequence of the misuse of your inner power. Come back to the one Truth, and realize that there is only One Spiritual Power, and It functions through the thoughts and images of your mind. The problems, vexations, and strife are due to the fact that man has actually wandered away after false Gods of fear and error. He must return to the center—the God-Presence within. Affirm now the sovereignty and authority of this Spiritual Power within you—the Principle of all life. Claim Divine guidance, strength, nourishment, and peace, and this Power will respond accordingly.

I will now proceed to point out how you may definitely and positively convey an idea or mental image to your subconscious mind. The conscious mind of man is personal and selective. It chooses, selects, weighs, analyzes, dissects, and investigates. It is capable of inductive and deductive reasoning. The subjective or subconscious mind is subject to the conscious mind. It might be called a servant of the conscious mind. The subconscious obeys the order of the conscious mind. Your conscious thought has power. The power you are acquainted with is thought. In the back of your thought is Mind, Spirit, or God. Focused, directed thoughts reach the subjective levels; they must be of a certain degree of intensity. Intensity is acquired by concentration.

To *concentrate* is to come back to the center and contemplate the Infinite Power within you that lies stretched in smiling repose. To concentrate properly, you still the wheels of your mind and enter into a quiet, relaxed mental state. When you concentrate, you gather your thoughts together, and you focus all your attention on your ideal, aim, or objective. You are now at a focal or central point, where you are giving all your attention and devotion to your mental image. The procedure of focused attention is somewhat similar to that of a magnifying glass, and the focus it makes of the rays of the sun. You can see the difference in the effect of scattered vibrations of the sun's heat, and the vibrations that emanate from a central point. You can direct the rays of the magnifying glass so that it will burn up a particular object upon which it is directed. Focused, steadied attention of your mental images gains a similar intensity; and a deep, lasting impression is made on the sensitive plate of the subconscious mind.

You may have to repeat this drama of the mind many times before an impression is made, but the secret of impregnating the deeper mind is continuous or sustained imagination. When fear or worry comes to you during the day, you can always immediately gaze upon that lovely picture in your mind, realizing and knowing that you have operated a definite psychological law that is now working for you in the dark house of your mind. As you do so, you are truly watering the seed and fertilizing it, thereby accelerating its growth.

The conscious mind of man is the motor; the subconscious is the engine. You must start the motor, and the engine will do the work. The conscious mind is the dynamo that awakens the power of the subconscious.

The first step in conveying your clarified desire, idea, or image to the deeper mind is to relax, immobilize the attention, and get still and quiet. This quiet, relaxed, peaceful attitude of mind prevents extraneous matter and false ideas from interfering with your mental absorption of your ideal; furthermore, in the quiet, passive, receptive attitude of mind, effort is reduced to a minimum.

In the second step, you begin to imagine the reality of that which you desire. For example, you may wish to sell a home. In private consultation with real estate brokers, I have told them of the way I sold my own home; they have applied it with remarkable results. I placed a sign in the garden in front of my home that read: "For sale by owner." The second day after placing the sign, I said to myself as I was going to sleep, "Supposing you sold the house, what would you do?"

I answered my own question, and I said, "I would take that sign down and throw it in the garage." In my imagination, I took hold of the sign, pulled it up from the ground, placed it on my shoulders, went to the garage, and threw it on the floor, saying jokingly to the sign, "I don't need you anymore!" I felt the inner satisfaction of it all, realizing that it *was* finished. The next day a man gave me a deposit of $1,000 and said, "Take your sign down; we will go into escrow now."

Immediately I pulled the sign up and took it into the garage. The outer action conformed to the inner. There is nothing new about this. "As within, so without," meaning according to the image impressed on the subconscious mind, so is it on the objective screen of your life.

This procedure or technique is older than our Bible. The outside mirrors the inside. External action follows internal action.

I was engaged by a very large organization to do some spiritual work for them. Through fraudulent means, others were trying to lay claim to their vast mining and other interests. They were harassing the company by legal trickery, and trying to get something for nothing. I told the lawyer to dramatize vividly in his imagination several times daily the president of the company that he represented congratulating him on the perfect, harmonious solution. As he sustained the mental picture, through continuous, mental application, the subjective wisdom gave him some new ideas—as he said, "Right out of the blue!" He followed these up, and the case was closed soon afterward.

If a person has a mortgage due at the bank, and he does not have the money to cover it, and if he will faithfully apply this principle, the subconscious mind will provide him with the money. Never mind, how, when, where, or through what source? The subjective mind has ways you know not of; its ways are past finding out. It is one of the instruments or tools that God gave man, so he could provide himself with all things necessary for his welfare. The man who hasn't the money to meet the mortgage can imagine himself depositing a check or currency required in the bank; that is, giving it to the cashier. The important point is to become intensely interested in the mental picture or imaginary act, making it real and natural. The more earnestly he engages his mind on the imaginary drama, the more effectually will the imaginary act be deposited in the bank of the subconscious mind. You can take a trip to the teller's window in your imagination, and make it so real and true that it will actually take place physically.

There is a young lady who comes to our Sunday-morning lectures regularly. She had to change buses three times; it took her one and one half hours each Sunday to come to the lectures. In the sermon, I told how a young man prayed for a car and received one. She went home and experimented as follows: Here is her letter, in part, published by her permission:

> *Dear Dr. Murphy:*
>
> *This is how I received a cadillac [sic]; I wanted one to come to the lectures on Sunday and Tuesdays. In my imagination I went through the identical process I would go through if I were actually driving a car. I went to the show room, and the salesman took me for a ride in one. I also drove it several blocks. I claimed the cadillac car as my own over and over again. I kept the mental picture of getting into the car, driving it, feeling the upholstery, etc., consistently for over two weeks. Last Sunday I drove to your meeting in a cadillac. My uncle in Inglewood passed away; left me his cadillac and his entire estate."*

If you are saying, well, I do not know of any way to get the money to pay off the mortgage, do not worry about it. *To worry* means to strangle. Realize that there is a Power inherent within you that can provide you with everything you need when you call upon It. You can decree now with feeling and conviction: "My house is free from all debt, and wealth flows to me in avalanches of abundance." Do not question the manner in which the answer to your prayer will come. You will do the obvious things necessary, knowing that the subconscious intelligence is directing all your steps, for it knows everything necessary for the fulfillment of your desires. You can also imagine a letter from the mortgage company informing you that you are paid up; rejoice in that image, and live with that imaginary letter in your mind until it becomes a conviction.

Become convinced now that there is a power within you that is capable of bringing what you imagine and feel as true into manifestation. Sitting idly by, daydreaming, and imagining the things you would like to possess, will not attract them to you. You must know and believe that you arc operating a law of mind; become convinced of your God-given power to use your mind constructively to bring into manifestation the thing you desire.

Know what you want. The subconscious mind will carry out the idea, because you have a definite,, clear-cut concept of what you wish to possess. Imagine clearly the fulfillment of your desire; then you are giving the subconscious something definite to act upon. The subconscious mind is the film upon which the picture is impressed. The subconscious develops the picture; and sends it back to you in a material, objectified form.

The camera is *you* consciously imagining the realization of your desire through focused attention. As you do this in a relaxed, happy mood, the picture is cast on the sensitive film of the subconscious mind. You also need a time exposure; it may be two or three minutes or longer depending on your temperament, feeling, and understanding. The important thing to remember is that it is not so much the time as the quality of your consciousness, degree of feeling, or faith. Generally speaking, the more focused and absorbed your attention is, and the longer the time, the more perfect will be the answer to your prayer. *Believe* that you have received, and ye shall receive. "Whatsoever ye shall ask in prayer, believing, ye shall receive." *To believe* is to accept something as true, or to live in the state of being it; as you sustain this mood, you shall experience the joy of the answered prayer!

CHAPTER THREE
How to Imagine Success

God is always successful in His undertakings. Man is equipped to succeed because God is within him. All the attributes, qualities, and potencies of God are within.

You were born to win, to conquer, and to overcome! The Intelligence, Wisdom, and Power of God are within you waiting to be released, and enabling you to rise above all difficulties.

There are many men who quietly use the abstract term *Success*, over and over many times a day until they reach a conviction that success *is* theirs. Remember that the *idea of success* contains all the essential elements of success. As man repeats the word *Success* to himself with faith and conviction, his subconscious mind will accept it as true of himself, and he will be under subjective compulsion to succeed.

We are compelled to express our subjective beliefs, impressions, and convictions. The ideal way to succeed is to know what you want to achieve. If you do not know your right place, or what you would like to do, you can ask for guidance on the question. The deeper mind will respond; as a result, you will find a push or tendency in a certain field of activity.

The deeper mind is responsive to your thought. The subconscious—sometimes called "subjective or deeper mind"—sets in operation its unconscious intelligence that attracts to the individual the conditions necessary for his success. Man should make it a special point to do the thing he loves to do. When you are happy in your endeavor, you are a success.

Accept the fact that you have an inner Creative Power. Let this be a positive conviction. This Infinite Power is responsive and reactive to your thought. To know, understand, and apply this principle causes doubt, fear, and worry to gradually disappear.

If a man dwells on the thought, for example, of failure, the thought of failure attracts failure. The subconscious takes the thought of failure as his request, and proceeds to make it manifest in his experience, because he indulges in the mental practice of conceiving failure. The subconscious mind is impersonal and non-selective.

A business friend of mine, a tailor by trade, has a favorite saying: "All I ever do is add. I never subtract." He means that *success* is a plus sign. *Add* to your growth, wealth, power, knowledge, faith, and wisdom.

Life is addition! Death is subtraction. You add to your life by imagining whatsoever things are true, lovely, noble, and Godlike. Imagine and feel yourself successful, and you must become successful. You arc never a slave to circumstances, environment, or conditions. You are master of conditions. You can become a victim of conditions by mentally acquiescing to things as they are. As you change your mind, you change conditions.

A movie actor told me once that he had very little education, but he had a dream as a boy of bring a successful movie actor. Out in the field mowing hay, or driving the cows home, or even when milking them, he said, "I would constantly imagine that I saw my name in big lights in a large theater. I kept this up for years until finally I ran away from home; got extra jobs in the motion picture field; and the day came when I saw my name in great big lights, as I did when I was a boy!" Then he added, "I know the power of *sustained* imagination to bring success."

What does *success* imply to you? You want undoubtedly to be successful in your relationship with others. You wish to be outstanding in your chosen work or profession. You wish to possess a beautiful home, and all the money you need to live comfortably and happily. You want to be successful in your prayers, and in your contact with the Universal Power within you.

Imagine yourself doing the thing you long to do, and possessing the things you long to possess. Become imaginative; mentally participate in the reality of the successful state; enter into that state of consciousness frequently; make a habit of it; then you will find you will be guided to do everything necessary for the realization of your dream. Go to sleep feeling successful every night and perfectly satisfied. You will succeed eventually in implanting the idea of success in your subconscious mind.

I know a drug clerk who was a licensed pharmacist receiving $40 a week plus his commission on sales. "After 25 years," he told me, "I will get a pension and retire."

I said to him, "Why don't you own your own store? Get out of this place. Raise your sights! Have a dream for your children. Maybe your son wants to be a doctor or your daughter desires to be a musician."

His answer was that he had no money! He began to awaken to the fact that whatever he could conceive as true, he could give it conception.

The first step toward your goal is the *birth of the idea* in the mind, and the second step is the *manifestation of the idea*. He began to imagine that he *was* in his own store. He participated in the act mentally. He arranged the bottles, dispensed prescriptions, and imagined several clerks in the store waiting on customers. He visualized a big bank balance. Mentally he worked in that imaginary store. Like a good actor, he lived the role. (Act as though I am, and I will be.) This drugstore clerk put himself wholeheartedly into the act . . . living, moving, and acting in the assumption that his store was his.

The sequel was interesting. He was discharged from his position, went with a large chain store, became manager, and then district manager. He made enough money in four years to make a down payment on a drugstore of his own. He called it his "dream pharmacy." "It was," he said, "exactly the store he saw in his imagination." He became successful in his chosen field, and was happy doing what he loved to do.

The individual who habitually maintains a mental attitude of faith and expectancy of the best is bound to succeed and advance in life. The individual who is depressed, dejected, morbid, and despondent attracts failure all along the line. Fear is truly a lack of faith in Divine supply. It is faith misplaced. Fear is faith in the wrong thing. Fear is a belief in lack, or that man's good is being withheld from him.

"Son, thou are ever with me, and all that I hath is thine." All things you need are in the invisible. It could be said that all things needed are in the abstract. You must desire to be greater than you are, in order to advance in life. Desire comes first, followed by a recognition of the Power within you enabling you to manifest what you want. The subconscious mind is the medium through which all that you desire can be brought into objectivity. You are the one giving orders in the form of habitual thinking, feeling, opinions, and beliefs. The subconscious mind obeys the orders given by the conscious mind. If your conscious mind is opposed to all negative thoughts, they can make no impression upon your subconscious mind. You become immunized.

If, for example, you say, "I wish I were healthy, then I could be much more successful in my work;" begin *now* to realize that your body is your mind expressed. The subconscious mind is the builder of the body, and controls all its vital functions. Your conscious mind has the power to change any idea or group of thoughts held in the subconscious mind. You can impress the idea of health on your subconscious mind when you know that it can be done. A conviction and sincere belief is necessary. Affirmative statements establish definite impression on the subconscious mind.

A wonderful way to impress the subconscious is through disciplined or scientific imagination. By illustration, if your knee is swollen and you are lame, imagine that you're doing the things you would do if you were in perfect health. You might say that I would go downtown on a bus, visit friends, ride horseback, go swimming, or hiking. First in your imagination you go on these psychological journeys, making them as real and natural as possible. *Continue* to go on these psychological journeys! You know that self-motivation is yours. All movement is first of the mind or consciousness of man before any external movement can take place.

By example, the chair does not move of itself. You must impart motion to it. The same is true of your body. As you continue to do all the things you would do were you healed, this inner movement will cause the subconscious to build the body in accordance with the image back of it.

The following is a wonderful prayer for perfect health. A minister I knew in South Africa applied this prayer and healed himself. Several times a day he would affirm slowly and quietly, first making certain that he was completely relaxed mentally and physically: "The perfection of God is now being expressed through me. The idea of health is now filling my subconscious mind. The image that God has of me is a perfect image, and my subconscious mind re-creates my body in perfect accordance with the perfect image held in the mind of God." This is a simple, easy way of conveying the idea of perfect health to your subconscious mind.

You can develop confidence by knowing and realizing that nothing can prevent you from achieving success. Develop a certainty in your mind that this Inner Power can be called upon to overcome all obstacles. There must be an assurance and determination on your part that you can achieve and accomplish what you set out to do. This positive, affirmative attitude constitutes confidence.

You have heard the Biblical expression: "According to your faith is it done unto you." Faith in God is the realization that there is only One Spiritual Power that is Omnipresent, Omniscient, Omnipotent, All Love, All Light, All Beauty, All Life, and An Ever-Present Help in time of trouble. Know that His Power responds to your thought.

Cease looking upon God as some Being living in the skies with a long beard. God is the Essence of man. God is the Life of man. We cannot comprehend all of God, for the finite mind cannot comprehend the Infinite en toto.

For example, your conscious and subconscious mind are projections of God; they are working tools. God is Infinite Wisdom, Boundless Love, Infinite Intelligence, Absolute Bliss, Eternal Harmony, and Indescribable Beauty. All these, and others, are Qualities and Attributes of God.

You are not cast adrift on the ocean of life deserted by the Creator of Life. This Presence and Power is within you. This Knowledge or Awareness of Divinity within you is the greatest and most powerful contributing factor to success.

Develop your talents; begin to use them; they are God-given. You have faculties and powers which require constant development.

"Man shall decree a thing, and it shall come to pass." What are you mentally decreeing now? What is the nature of your inner talking, inner conversation, and your idle moods? Man shall account for every idle word he speaks. The idle words are doubt, fear, anxiety, and worry. If these are present, you are not giving definite, positive orders to your subconscious mind, because there is no definite impression made as to what you wish to bring to pass.

Fear and worry cause confusion in the conscious mind. This creates confusion in the subconscious mind, and nothing happens but confusion in man's affairs. Continue to trust in the Divine Power, and that which you desire will come to you in some manner. Have faith in God, in the Divine Power, in His Divine Love, and His Overshadowing Presence always watching over you, and you will become invincible. "Trust in the Lord and do good; *so* shalt thou dwell in the land, and verily thou shalt be fed."

How to Prosper

How to
Prosper

Dr. Joseph Murphy

"Man shall not live by bread alone, but by every word that proceedeth out of the mouth of God."

—(MATTHEW 4:4).

The law of abundance is expressed simply by the Psalmist when he says, "His delight is in the law of the Lord." When our pleasure and our desire are for the "law of the Lord," and when we yearn for the vision and the practice of the understanding of the law of harmony and perfection, we are on the way to health, peace, and abundance. Let us merge in feeling with the One Who Forever Is; then we shall bring forth fruit in due season; we shall find that Christ-like plans and opportunities will present themselves to us and our leaf (ideas) also shall not wither. Whatever we undertake and whatever presents itself, we shall fulfill and execute; moreover whatever fire, energy, and enthusiasm we need to bring forth our ideal, spring from the heavenly tree, and are watered by the heavenly waters of love and faith.

Prosperity means to increase our capacity or ability in every direction, so that we make use of ourselves and the Power. The American mind connects the word *prosper* with a dollar bill, but we do not get more money until we prosper inwardly by increasing our knowledge of God, the way He works, and by deepening our ability to express ourselves.

We never pray for things; we enter into a state of consciousness of *being* or *having* our desire The position, money, and connection you wish to make are the images, likenesses, or physical forms of the states of consciousness which produce them.

The money, friends, etc., you desire can be manifested by entering into the *feeling of having* what you long to possess. Feast in this mood until you are *filled full* of the feeling of being it; continue until your desire has passed away, and you are at peace. "*I am the bread of Life.*" (John 6:35). Let us realize that I Am is the true bread. When you say, "I will be, maybe, and perhaps," you are claiming and stating your lack. You are admitting, "I do not have."

Let us dwell on the truth propounded by Jesus when he said, "*whatsoever ye shall ask in prayer, believing, ye shall receive.*" (Matthew 21:22). If you claim in the silence, "I am wealthy," these words will not produce wealth. We must *feel* wealthy. The consciousness of wealth produces wealth. We must know that we are here to dramatize, portray, and express God, which is harmony, health, and peace. Our lives should be full of joyous experiences; we should develop freely along all lines.

This whole law of prosperity is condensed beautifully in the words: *"Give us this day our daily bread."* (Matthew 6:11). Infinite supply and substance are omnipresent; we must accept this fact in the same manner that we accept the luscious fruit off the trees in the orchard; we must put up our hand and take the fruit off the trees; similarly, we must claim supply and acknowledge its presence.

Money is a medium of exchange, a token, or symbol. It is an idea in Divine Mind. There is no shortage of air or sunshine; likewise, there is no shortage of supply. What is the capacity of our lungs when we imbibe air? This amount is all we can inhale in one breath. In the same manner let us ask ourselves, "What is my capacity to receive?"

By illustration, we may want some water at the seashore. If we take a wine glass to the ocean, we can only receive that measure; some people take a gallon; others a demi-john, but they can never exhaust the ocean; there is enough for all. The Source of all of our good is the one unchangeable Spirit, which is inexhaustible and omnipresent.

If you think that your good and supply are dependent upon a certain position, you are wrong. The job is merely the channel through which your supply may come, and God's channels are infinite. When one door closes, another one opens.

What should be one's attitude if one has lost one's position due to the fact that one's employer became bankrupt? Instead of bemoaning the loss, that person should rejoice and say inwardly that a new, wonderful position will be instantly available; then a new position and a better one will come in an easy manner. Let us become indifferent to the channel, and become conscious of the Source of our good; daily unite with the First Cause in right thinking, right feeling, and right action.

We must feel the Presence of God; this is an experience in our own consciousness. It is all very well to theorize about the Presence and to think about Him, but we must also have the inner realization that comes through communing in the silence every morning and night of each day. Meditate on the attributes and qualities of the Deity, and you will feel the Presence welling up within you spontaneously. You do not see or smell the wind; you feel the breeze upon your face; likewise, you can feel the warmth and the glow of the Presence. Some people refer to it as a tingling sensation; it is as if the melody of the Gods were playing on the sacral plexus.

If you wish to demonstrate prosperity, forget the past; yesterday is dead; however, we can make it alive today by thinking and dwelling on it. Nothing lives but today's mood or feeling; it is your mood that demonstrates. It is idle and foolish for people to spend their time and energy dwelling upon how wealthy they were at one time. Frequently they say, "Why can't I demonstrate *now?*" The reason is that to dwell on the past is death and stagnation. Let us by all means rejoice in our demonstrations in the past, but "Now is the accepted time; behold *now* is the day of salvation."

Infinite supply is instantly available *now.* Regardless of what you had or lost in the past, supply is awaiting your claim and recognition. This supply is omnipresent; it is never conditioned by the ebb and flow of your apprehension. You cannot eat last week's food today. Accept your good now, and walk in the assumption that "It is done."

Scientific thinkers or truth students are never envious or jealous of another, because they know they can go to the same Fountain and ask for anything they want. When we are jealous of the wealth and success of the other, it holds us back and prevents us from demonstrating prosperity. It raises the other person and lowers us. The Law is no respecter of persons; it gives to all according to their belief. Envy is a waste of energy and a destructive, emotional force. Let us rejoice on the success of the other; then we attract success to ourselves. We must realize that the other person is an extension of ourselves.

We can find our true place in life by claiming and feeling Infinite Spirit has revealed it to us, and that we are now expressing our hidden talents to the world. As we continue to claim and accept this in consciousness, we will be divinely led to our true place in life. The God within will automatically give whatever we need for this expression to us. We will never be successful until we find the work we love to do. When we love the thing we are doing, it is no longer drudgery; neither are we any longer working by the sweat of our brow. The latter concept is the customary one, but it is definitely wrong. "They rest and their works do follow." You and God are one in the work that you are doing.

When you are expressing your talents to the world, blessing, and benefiting your compatriots, you may rest assured that you are doing your Father's business. If you are in the Master's business or any part of it, God by his very nature is for you, so who can be against you? With this attitude of mind there is no power in heaven or earth to withhold success from you.

There are times when people come to me and say, "Times are very slow; real estate is not moving." Real estate—like anything else—is an idea in Divine

Mind; all that the owners have to do is to exchange ideas with others. Buying and selling take place in our own consciousness. If you have something to sell, feel and know that Infinite Spirit has now revealed to you the right person at the right time, and that the sale is already accomplished in the Kingdom of Reality. Your feeling or conviction that the transaction has already taken place in your consciousness, the only true medium of exchange, gives you confidence and trust. You wait for just a little while and the answer comes—sometimes as a thief in the night, as a surprise, or when you least expect it.

Always remember that Infinite Wisdom has the *know how* of accomplishment; so if you desire a change and wish to sell your property, some merchandise or an idea to another, this Being knows the perfect answer to all of your requests. If the person who would be blessed and made happy by your idea is in China, he or she would be brought back, and you would be irresistibly attracted to one another. "My ways are past finding out."

Many people ask, "Can I, or should I, get $150,000 for my property?" The answer is in the question. The golden rule is the law of life; all else is commentary. If the tables were reversed, would you be willing to pay $150,000 yourself? Are you at ease in your own consciousness regarding the price? Is it just and equitable in your eyes? If you can answer these questions in the affirmative, the price is right.

In all of our transactions let us remember the Golden Rule: "Do unto others as you would have others do unto you."

When we have property to sell, do we inwardly feel we are over-charging? Are we clever in deceiving the other? Do we try to take advantage of the other person by subterfuge or underhand methods? If we do, we are using the law in reverse. We truly prosper when we use the law righteously. When we rob, steal, and cheat, we have a fear and guilt complex; we attract loss to ourselves. "For there is nothing covered, that shall not be revealed" (Luke 12:2). There is a principle of justice, in the same manner as there is a principle of mathematics.

I have talked with many people over a period of years, and a frequent complaint is, "If you saw all of the bills that I have to meet—times are terrible!" We must realize that there are no debts in Heaven (harmony). How is it in God and Heaven?

The answer is that bliss, harmony, perfect equilibrium, and joy are the states of consciousness called heaven. Let us realize that all bills are now paid; rejoice that it is so. Let us mark them paid in our own minds by entering into the joyous, happy state that all bills are paid, and drop off to sleep with the words, "Thank you,

Father" on our lips. We are giving thanks for the gift already received in consciousness. We give the gift to ourselves by an inner awareness, feeling, or conviction. In some way all of these bills will be paid; there will also be a divine surplus. We can now decree that we are one with the Infinite Source of supply, and that all of our needs are met instantly; then watch the Law work!

If you want money, be friendly with money; then you will never lack it. When money is in circulation, times are prosperous. When people begin to brood and worry, fear—the ugly monster—raises its head and a depression sets in. It is all purely psychological. There is no shortage in nature. Nature is lavish, extravagant, and bountiful. It has been said that the amount of fruit that falls to the ground and rots in the tropics every year would feed the whole world. The shortage and the lack come, because of our failures in distribution and abuse of nature's bounty.

The book entitled *Suggestion and Auto-suggestion* by Charles Baudouin and Eden Paul (Dobb-Mead, 1921) brought to the attention of the world The Law of Reversed Effort. On page 137 in the Chapter entitled Laws of Suggestion it states: "When an idea imposes itself on the mind to such an extent as to give rise to a suggestion, all the conscious efforts which the subject makes in order to counteract this suggestion are not merely without the desired effect, but they actually run counter to the subject's conscious wishes and tend to intensify the suggestion." In other words, whenever we are in a doubtful, confused state of mind, and are saying to ourselves, "I should like to, but I cannot," or "I want money to pay my bills, but it is hopeless," we may wish as hard as we please, but the harder we try, the less able we are to manifest our desire.

When we are in financial difficulty, many noxious suggestions present themselves, such as: fear, despair, and a complete lack of faith. We becomes perplexed and feel lost. The harder we try to think the good idea, the more violent is the assault of the bad idea.) Effort is not the way to obtain the desired results.

Emile Coué originated the *Law of Reversed Effort.* This is Coué's formula in his own words: "When the will and the imagination are at war, the imagination invariably gains the say." Another way of stating it is, when our desire is in conflict with our imagination or belief, our belief wins. The dominant idea always wins. Effort presupposes the idea of resistance that is to be overcome; thus we have two conflicting ideas or suggestions: "I want wealth or money now, but I cannot get it." Neutralization takes place and nothing happens. It is like mixing an acid and an alkali; the result is an inert substance.

When we say, "I prayed for abundance and for supply *so hard,*" we relate the major error of this type of thinking. The way to success is *effortless* and without any struggle. An effortless way is brought about by the sleeping technique as suggested by a movement called "The New Nancy School" in 1910. "We must be careful to note that immobilization of the attention, if it is to produce its proper effect, must be carried out with no sense of strain; we must be able to maintain it with the minimum of voluntary effort." The condition is analogous to the experience in which people often find themselves on first waking in the morning; they say to themselves that they could get up if they liked, but almost against their will they continue to snuggle under the blankets. In Baudouin and Paul's book, this is explained: "A very simple way of securing this" (impregnation of the subconscious) "is to condense the idea which is to be the object of the suggestion, to sum it up in a brief phrase which can readily be graven on the memory, and to repeat it over and over again like a lullaby."

These authors convey that when we enter into the sleepy state, or as they describe it, "the state akin to sleep," (between the waking and sleeping state) effort is reduced to a minimum, and we can focus our attention on our good with ease and without strain. We can induce the sleepy state by suggesting sleep to ourselves.

Let us give a practical application of the above teaching. A woman in my class last year said, "Bills are piling up; I am out of work; I have three children and no money, what shall I do?" This is what she did: She relaxed her body in an arm chair; entered into the sleepy state, and as Coué suggested, she condensed the ideas of her needs into the three words, "It is done." The significance of these words to her meant the realization of all of her desires, such as: all bills paid, a new position, a home, a husband, food and clothing for the children, and an ample supply of money.

Note the logic of the accepted prayer in the condensed phrase, "It is done," which was repeated over and over again like a lullaby as suggested by that famous New Nancy School. Each time she silently pronounced, "It is done," a feeling of warmth and peace stole over her, until she reached the point of conviction that it was finished. Her mind did not wander, because she focused and concentrated on one central idea; she repeated it over and over again until it had the feeling of reality.

When we restrict our attention upon one simple phrase, it prevents the mind from wandering through the associational network of ideas and thoughts. If the mind wanders, bring it back and have it continue to repeat the short phrase that means to you the *realization* of all of your dreams. God's ways are truly past finding out! If I go to a fountain, and I do not have any bucket, I cannot get water; likewise, when I go to the fountain of living waters within me, I must have a bucket, which is my receptive attitude of mind when I am in a passive, receptive, joyous state, the single idea or feeling of thankfulness dominates.

Let us cite the case of a man who was having difficulty selling his property; he was very poor. He reclined in a chair; closed his eyes, and immobilized his attention by feeling sleepy. As he became relaxed, he entered that drowsy, sleepy state as we have suggested; it favors results because effort is reduced. *Prayer should be effortless effort.* He selected the condensed phrase, "Thank you"; he repeated it, as if he was addressing the Supreme Being for having accomplished the sale for him. He did not fall asleep the minute he closed his eyes, but he was alert, alive, and quickened by the Holy Spirit; he entered the silence with an expectant attitude; he knew that he was going to receive his desire.

He silently repeated, "Thank you," over and over again like a lullaby; he continued to speak these words until he had the feeling that all was We are reminded of the thankful, Christ-like attitude of mind found in Jesus' words: *"Father, I thank thee that thou hast heard me, and I knew that thou hearest me always."* (John 11:41–42) He fell asleep; in a dream (fourth dimensional world) he saw a man who gave him a check, and he said to the man, "Thank you, Father"; then he awakened; he knew that the property was sold. In a week's time that man whom he saw in the dream came to him, and bought the property, which consisted of fourteen lots, a well and a home.

The reason for this fourth dimensional experience was that he continued to repeat the words, "Thank you," until he fell into the deep of sleep. In the next dimension—where we go every night as we fall asleep—he saw the desired transaction as a concrete, objective fact. The *now* or the *present* in the fourth dimension is equivalent to *here* in the third dimension. Having seen it fourth dimensionally, we must experience it in the future in the third dimensional plane.

Decree silently night and morning that God is prospering you in mind, body, and affairs; *feel* the reality of it, and you will never want for anything. Repeat over and over again like a lullaby, "Thank you, Father," as you prepare for sleep; this means you are thanking your Higher Self for abundance, health, and harmony. Truly God will make Himself known to you in a vision, and He will speak to you in a dream.

If you are married, take this wonderful opportunity of agreeing on the law of abundance; it is an ever-flowing, omnipresent supply of God's goodness, truth, and beauty. Let husband and wife agree and unite their ideals and motives in the demonstration for abundance along all lines.

Many of the greatest people in all walks of life have been inspired by their spouses. Married people can see each other, as they ought to be. Right feeling and inner knowing can transform defeat into success and poverty into abundance. Together they become a driving power and powerful motive for the demonstration of abundance achieving their agreement with God. The awareness that "I and the Father are One," is the state of consciousness that is the answer. The two agreeing or touching on anything can be husband and wife. "If God be for us, who shall be against us?" "One with God is a majority." "All things are possible with God."

Summary

To develop the abundant life, meditate on the meaning and substance of the words of the first Psalm: Blessed is the man that walketh not in the counsel of the ungodly, nor standeth in the way of sinners, nor sitteth in the seat of the scornful.

But his delight is in the law of the Lord; and in his law Both he meditate day and night.

And he shall be like a tree planted by the rivers of water that bringeth forth his fruit in his season; his leaf also shall not wither; and whatsoever he doeth shall prosper.

The ungodly are not so: but are like the chaff which the wind driveth away.

Therefore the ungodly shall not stand in the judgment, nor sinners in the congregation of the righteous.

For the Lord knoweth the way of the righteous: but the way of the ungodly shall perish.

Meditations &
Affirmations

Meditations & Affirmations

For Health, Wealth, Relationships, and Self-Expression

Dr. Joseph Murphy

Contents

INTRODUCTION

These pages are full of powerful affirmations for Health, Wealth, Relationships, and Self-Expression. The idea behind these techniques is pretty simple. Most of us grow up learning to put ourselves down for any real or imagined error. We grow up believing certain things about ourselves or comparing ourselves negatively to others. The use of positive affirmations is a technique to change negative self-talk into something more positive. Since we've spent many years on the negative image it's unreasonable to expect an instant effect from affirmations, but if we stick to it for a few days, with honesty, trust, and belief, results will start to happen.

Consciousness of Health

- ❦ How to Apply the Healing Principle
- ❦ The Healing Principle
- ❦ Wearing His Garment
- ❦ The Quiet Mind
- ❦ Mental Poise
- ❦ The Peace of God
- ❦ Spiritual Medicine
- ❦ Controlling My Emotions
- ❦ Overcoming Fear
- ❦ The Holy Temple

How To Apply The Healing Principle

I WILL RESTORE health unto thee, and I will heal thee of thy wounds, say the Lord. The God in me has limitless possibilities. I know that all things are possible with God. I believe this and accept it wholeheartedly now. I know that the God-Power in me makes darkness light and crooked things straight. I am now lifted up in consciousness by contemplating that God indwells me.

I speak the word now for the healing of mind, body, and affairs; I know that this Principle within me responds to my faith and trust. "The Father does the works." I am now in touch with life, love, truth, and beauty within me. I now align myself with the Infinite Principle of Love and Life within me. I know that harmony, health, and peace are now being expressed in my body.

As I live, move, and act in the assumption of my perfect health, it becomes actual. I now imagine and feel the reality of my perfect body. I am filled with a sense of peace and well-being. Thank you, Father.

THE HEALING PRINCIPLE

Jesus said, "Thy faith hath made thee whole."

I positively believe in the Healing Power of God within me. My conscious and subconscious minds are in perfect agreement. I accept the statement of truth which I positively affirm. The words I speak are words of spirit and they are truth.

I now decree that the healing Power of God is transforming my whole body making me whole, pure, and perfect. I believe with a deep, inner certitude that my prayer of faith is being manifest now. I am guided by the wisdom of God in all matters. The Love of God flows in transcendent beauty and loveliness into my mind and body, transforming, normalizing, and energizing every atom of my being. I sense the peace that passes through understanding. God's Glory surrounds me, and I rest forever in the Everlasting Arms.

WEARING HIS GARMENT

I have found God in the sanctuary of my own soul. God is Life; that Life is my life. I know God is not a body; He is shapeless, timeless, and ageless; I see God in my mind's eye. Through understanding I see and look upon God in the same way that I see the answer to a mathematical problem.

I now rise to the awareness of peace, poise, and power. This feeling of joy, peace, and goodwill within me is actually the spirit of God moving within me; It is God in action; It is Almighty. There is no power in external things to hurt me; the only Power re-sides in my own mind and consciousness.

My body is the garment of God. The Living Spirit Almighty is within me; It is absolutely pure, holy, and perfect. I know that this Holy Spirit is God, and that this Spirit is now flowing through me healing and making my body whole, pure, and perfect. I have complete power over my body and my world.

My thoughts of peace, power, and health have the Power of God to be realized within me now. "Blessed are the pure in heart: for they shall see God." I have seen and felt His Holy Presence; it is wonderful.

THE QUIET MIND

God dwells at the center of my being. God is Peace; this Peace enfolds me in Its Arms now. There is a deep feeling of security, vitality, and strength underlying this peace. This inner sense of peace, in which I now dwell, is the silent, brooding Presence of God. The Love and the Light of God watch over me, as a loving mother watches over the sleeping child. Deep in my heart is the Holy Presence that is my peace, my strength, and my source of supply.

All fear has vanished. I see God in all people; I see God manifest in all things. I am an instrument of the Divine Presence. I now release this inner peace; it flows through my entire being releasing and dissolving all problems; this is the peace that passes through understanding.

MENTAL POISE

"Whither shall I go from thy Spirit? Or whither shall I flee from thy Presence? If I ascend up into heaven, thou art there: if I make my bed in hell, behold, thou art there. If I take the wings of the morning, and dwell in the uttermost parts of the sea: Even there shall thy hand lead me, and thy right hand shall hold me." I am now full of a Divine enthusiasm, because I am in the Presence of Divinity. I am in the Presence of All Power, Wisdom, Majesty, and Love.

The Light of God illumines my intellect; my mind is full of poise, balance, and equilibrium. There is a perfect mental adjustment to all things. I am at peace with my own thoughts. I rejoice in my work; it gives me joy and happiness. I draw continually upon my Divine Storehouse; for It is the only Presence and the only Power. My mind is God's mind; I am at peace.

THE PEACE OF GOD

All is peace and harmony in my world, for God in me is "The Lord of Peace." I am the consciousness of God in action; I am always at peace. My mind is poised, serene, and calm. In this atmosphere of peace and goodwill which surrounds me, I feel a deep abiding strength and freedom from all fear. I now sense and feel the love and beauty of His Holy Presence. Day by day I am more aware of God's Love; all that is false falls away. I see God personified in all people. I know that as I allow this inner peace to flow through my being, all problems are solved. I dwell in God; therefore, I rest in the eternal arms of peace. "Your life is hid with Christ in God." My peace is the deep, unchanging peace of God; "It is the peace of God, which passes through all understanding."

SPIRITUAL MEDICINE

"A merry heart makes a cheerful countenance." The spirit of the Almighty pervades every atom of my being making me whole, joyous, and perfect. I know that all of the functions of my body respond to this inner joy welling up within me. I am now stirring up the gift of God within me; I feel wonderful. The oil of joy and illumination anoint my intellect, and become a lamp unto my feet.

I am now perfectly adjusted emotionally; there is a Divine equilibrium functioning in my mind, body, and affairs. I resolve from this moment forward to express peace and happiness to every person I meet. I know that my happiness and peace come from God; as I shed His light, love, and truth to others, I am also blessing and healing myself in countless ways. I radiate the sunshine of God's Love to all mankind. His Light shines through me and illuminates my path. I am resolved to express peace, joy, and happiness.

CONTROLLING MY EMOTIONS

When a negative thought of fear, jealousy, or resentment enters my mind, I supplant it with the thought of God. My thoughts are God's thoughts, and God's Power is with my thoughts of good. I know I have complete dominion over my thoughts and emotions. I am a channel of the Divine. I now redirect all of my feelings and emotions along harmonious, constructive lines. "The sons of God shouted for joy." I now rejoice to accept the ideas of God which are peace, harmony, and goodwill, and I delight to ex-press them; this heals all discord within me. Only God's ideas enter my mind, bringing me harmony, health, and peace. God is Love. Perfect Love casts out fear, resentment, and all negative states. I now fall in love with truth. I wish for all men everything I wish for myself; I radiate love, peace, and good will to all. I am at peace.

OVERCOMING FEAR

There is no fear, as "perfect Love casts out fear." Today I permit Love to keep me in perfect harmony and peace with all levels of my world. My thoughts are loving, kind, and harmonious. I sense my oneness with God, for "In Him I live, move, and have my being."

I know that all of my desires will be realized in perfect order. I trust the Divine Law within me to bring my ideals to pass. "The Father does the works." I am divine, spiritual, joyous, and absolutely fearless. I am now surrounded by the perfect peace of God; it is "The peace of God which passes through all understanding." I now place all of my attention on the thing desired. I love this desire, and I give it my whole-hearted attention.

My spirit is lifted into the mood of confidence and peace; this is the spirit of God moving in me. It gives me a sense of peace, security, and rest. Truly, "perfect Love casts out fear."

THE HOLY TEMPLE

"Those that be planted in the house of the LORD shall flourish in the courts of our God." I am still and at peace. My heart and my mind are motivated by the spirit of goodness, truth, and beauty. My thought is now on the Presence of God within me; this stills my mind.

I know that the way of creation is Spirit moving upon its self. My True Self now moves in and on It-self creating peace, harmony, and health in my body and affairs. I am Divine in my deeper self. I know I am a son of the living God; I create the way God creates by the self-contemplation of spirit. I know my body does not move of itself. It is acted upon by my thoughts and emotions.

I now say to my body, "Be still and quiet." It must obey. I understand this and I know it is a Divine Law. I take my attention away from the physical world; I feast in the House of God within me. I meditate and feast upon harmony, health, and peace; these come forth from the God- Essence within; I am at peace. My body is a temple of the Living God. "God is in His Holy Temple; let all the earth keep silent before Him.

ACCEPT ABUNDANCE

- ❦ God is the Eternal Now
- ❦ The Way of Prayer
- ❦ How to Realize the Abundant Life
- ❦ The Prayer of Faith
- ❦ The Abundant Life
- ❦ Imagination, the Workshop of God
- ❦ God's Will For Me
- ❦ Abide in the Silence
- ❦ To Be, To Do, and To Have

GOD IS THE ETERNAL NOW

(Using the Subconscious Mind)
KNOW THAT MY GOOD is this very moment. I believe in my heart that I can prophesy for myself har-

mony, health, peace, and joy. I enthrone the concept of peace, success, and prosperity in my mind now. I know and believe these thoughts (seeds) will grow and manifest themselves in my experience.

I am the gardener; as I sow, so shall I reap. I sow God-like thoughts (seeds); these wonderful seeds are peace, success, harmony, and goodwill. It is a wonderful harvest.

From this moment forward I am depositing in the Universal Bank (my subconscious mind) seeds or thoughts of peace, confidence, poise, and balance. I am drawing out the fruit of the wonderful seeds I am depositing. I believe and accept the fact that my desire is a seed deposited in the subconscious. I make it real by feeling the reality of it. I accept the reality of my desire in the same manner I accept the fact that the seed deposited in the ground will grow. I know it grows in the darkness; also, my desire or ideal grows in the darkness of my subconscious mind; in a little while, like the seed, it comes above the ground (becomes objectified) as a condition, circumstance, or event.

Infinite Intelligence governs and guides me in all ways. I meditate on whatsoever things are true, honest, just, lovely, and of good report. I think on these things, and God's Power is with my thoughts of Good. I am at peace.

THE WAY OF PRAYER

"Thou shell make thy way prosperous, and then thou shell have good success." I now give a pattern of success and prosperity to the deep mind within me, which is the law. I now identify myself with the Infinite Source of supply. I listen to the still, small voice of God within me. This inner voice leads, guides, and governs all of my activities. I am one with the abundance of God. I know and believe that there are new and better ways of conducting my business; In-finite Intelligence reveals the new ways to me.

I am growing in wisdom and understanding. My business is God's business. I am divinely prospered in all ways. Divine Wisdom within me reveals the ways and means by which all of my affairs are adjusted in the right way immediately.

The words of faith and conviction which I now speak open up all the necessary doors or avenues for my success and prosperity. I know that "The Lord (Law) will perfect that which concerns me." My feet are kept in the perfect path, because I am a son of the living God.

HOW TO REALIZE THE ABUNDANT LIFE

I know that to prosper means to grow spiritually along all lines. God is prospering me now in mind, body, and affairs. God's ideas constantly unfold with-in me bringing to me health, wealth, and perfect Divine expression.

I thrill inwardly as I feel the Life of God vitalizing every atom of my being. I know that God's Life is animating, sustaining, and strengthening me now. I am now expressing a perfect, radiant body full of vitality, energy, and power.

My business or profession is a Divine activity, and since it is God's business, it is successful and prosperous. I imagine and feel an inner wholeness functioning through my body, mind, and affairs. I give thanks, and rejoice in the abundant life.

THE PRAYER OF FAITH

"The prayer of faith shall save the sick man, and God shall raise him up." I know that no matter what the negation of yesterday was, that my prayer or affirmation of truth will rise triumphantly over it today. I steadfastly behold the joy of the answered prayer. I walk all day long in the Light.

Today is God's day; it is a glorious day for me, as it is full of peace, harmony, and joy. My faith in the good is written in my heart and felt in my in-ward parts. I am absolutely convinced that there is a Presence and a perfect Law which receives the impress of my desire now, and which irresistibly attracts into my experience all the good things my heart desires. I now place all of my reliance, faith, and trust in the Power and Presence of God within me; I am at peace.

I know I am a guest of the Infinite, and that God is my Host. I hear the invitation of the Holy One saying, "Come unto me all ye that labor, and I will give you rest." I rest in God; all is well.

THE ABUNDANT LIFE

"Consider the Lilies of the field; they toil not, neither do they spin; yet Solomon in all of his glory was not arrayed as one of these." I know that God is prospering me in all ways. I am now leading the abundant life, because I believe in a God of abundance. I am supplied with everything that contributes to my beauty, well being, progress, and peace. I am daily experiencing the fruits of the spirit of God within me; I accept my good now; I walk in the light that all good is mine. I am peaceful, poised, serene, and calm. I am one with the source of life; all of my needs are met at every moment of time and every point of space. I now bring "all the empty vessels" to the Father within. The fullness of God is made manifest in all of the departments of my life. "All that the Father hath is mine." I rejoice that this is so.

IMAGINATION, THE WORKSHOP OF GOD

"Where there is no vision, the people perish." My vision is that I desire to know more of God, and the way He works. My vision is for perfect health, harmony, and peace. My vision is the inner faith that Infinite Spirit heals and guides me now in all ways. I know and believe that the God-Power within me answers my prayer; this is a deep conviction within me.

I know that imagination is the result of what I image in my mind. "Faith is," as Paul says, "the substance out of which the image is formed."

I make it my daily practice to imagine only for myself and others that which is noble, wonderful, and Christ-like. I now imagine that I am doing the thing I long to do; I imagine that I now possess the things I long to possess; I imagine I am what I long to be. To make it real, I feel the reality of it; I know that it is so. Thank you, Father.

GOD'S WILL FOR ME

"God opens for me the windows of heaven, and pours me out a blessing."

God's will must be God-like; for that is the nature of God. God's will for me, therefore, is health, goodness, harmony, and abundance.

"If ye abide in me, and my words abide in you, ye shall ask what ye will, and it shall be done unto you." I am now enlightened by the truth; each day I am growing in wisdom and understanding. I am a perfect channel for the works of God; I am free from all worry and confusion. Infinite Intelligence within me is a lamp unto my feet. I know I am led to do the right thing; for it is God in action in all of my affairs.

The peace that passes understanding fills my mind now. I believe and accept my ideal. I know it subsists in the Infinite. I give it form and expression by my complete mental acceptance. I feel the reality of the fulfilled desire. The peace of God fills my soul.

ABIDE IN SILENCE

Jesus said, "God is a Spirit: and they that worship him must worship him in spirit and in truth." I know and realize that God is a spirit moving within me. I know that God is a feeling or deep conviction of harmony, health, and peace within me; it is the movement of my own heart. The spirit or feeling of confidence and faith which now possesses me is the spirit of God and the action of God on the waters of my mind; this is God; it is the creative Power within me. I live, move, and have my being in the faith and confidence that goodness, truth, and beauty shall follow me all of the days of my life; this faith in God and all things good is omnipotent; it removes all barriers. I now close the door of the senses; I withdraw all attention from the world. I turn within to the One, the Beautiful, and the Good; here, I dwell with my Father beyond time and space; here, I live, move, and dwell in the shadow of the Almighty. I am free from all fear, from the verdict of the world, and the appearance of things. I now feel His Presence which is the feeling of the answered prayer, or the presence of my good. I become that which I contemplate. I now feel that I am what I want to be; this feeling or awareness is the action of God in me; it is the creative Power. I give thanks for the joy of the answered prayer, and I rest in the silence that "It is done."

TO BE, TO DO, AND TO HAVE

At the center of my being is Peace; this is the peace of God. In this stillness I feel strength, guidance, and the Love of His Holy Presence. I am divinely active; I am expressing the fullness of God along all lines. I am a channel for the Divine, and I now release the imprisoned splendor that is within. I am divinely guided to my true expression in life; I am compensated in a wonderful way. I see God in everything and personified in all men everywhere. I know as I permit this river of peace to flow through my being, all of my problems are solved. All things I need to fully express myself on this plane are irresistibly attracted to me by the Universal Law of attraction. The way is revealed to me; I am full of joy and harmony.

Love, Personality, Human, and Family Relationships

- ❦ God's Broadcast
- ❦ Spiritual Rebirth
- ❦ Love Frees
- ❦ The Secret Place
- ❦ Control Your Emotions
- ❦ Prayer of Gratitude
- ❦ How to Attract Your Divine Companion
- ❦ How to Pray for Companionship
- ❦ Divine Freedom
- ❦ Prayer for Peace

GOD'S BROADCAST

"ALL YE ARE BRETHREN, for one is your father."

I always bring harmony, peace, and joy into every situation and into all of my personal relationships. I know, believe, and claim that the peace of God reigns supreme in the mind and heart of everyone in my home and business. No matter what the problem is, I always maintain peace, poise, patience, and wisdom. I fully and freely forgive everyone, regardless of what they may have said or done. I cast all of my burdens on the Christ within; I go free; this is a marvelous feeling. I know that blessings come to me as I forgive.

I see the angel of God's Presence behind every problem or difficult situation. I know the solution is there, and that everything is working out in Divine order. I trust the God-Presence implicitly; it has the know-how of accomplishment. The Absolute Order of Heaven and His Absolute Wisdom are acting through me now and at all times; I know that order is Heaven's first law. My mind is now fixed joyously and expectantly on this perfect harmony. I know the result is the inevitable, perfect solution; my answer is God's answer; it is Divine; for it is the melody of God's broadcast.

SPIRITUAL REBIRTH

Today I am reborn spiritually! I completely detach myself from the old way of thinking, and I bring

Divine love, light, and truth definitely into my experience. I consciously feel love for everyone I meet. Mentally I say to everyone I contact, "I see the Christ in you, and I know you see the Christ in me." I recognize the qualities of God in everyone. I practice this morning, noon, and night; it is a living part of me.

I am reborn spiritually now, because all day long I practice the Presence of God. No matter what I am doing—whether I am walking the street, shopping, or about my daily business—whenever my thought wanders away from God or the good, I bring it back to the contemplation of His Holy Presence. I feel noble, dignified, and Christ-like. I walk in a high mood sensing my oneness with God. His peace fills my soul.

LOVE FREES

God is Love, and God is Life; this Life is one and indivisible. Life manifests itself in and through all people; It is at the center of my own being.

I know that light dispels the darkness, so does the love of the good overcome all evil. My knowledge of the power of Love overcomes all negative conditions now. Love and hate cannot dwell together. I now turn the Light of God upon all fear or anxious thoughts in my mind, and they flee away. The dawn (light of truth) appears and the shadows (fear and doubt) flee away.

I know Divine Love watches over me, guides me, and makes clear the path for me. I am expanding into the Divine. I am now expressing God in all of my thoughts, words, and actions; the nature of God is Love. I know that "perfect Love casteth out fear."

THE SECRET PLACE

"He that dwelled in the secret place of the most high shall abide under the shadow of the Almighty."

I dwell in the secret place of the most high; this is my own mind. All of my thoughts entertained by me conform to harmony, peace, and goodwill. My mind is the dwelling place of happiness, joy, and a deep sense of security. All of the thoughts that enter my mind contribute to my joy, peace, and general welfare. I live, move, and have my being in the atmosphere of good fellowship, love, and unity.

All of the people that dwell in my mind are God's children. I am at peace in my mind with all of the members of my household and all mankind. The same good I wish for myself, I wish for all men. I am living in the house of God now. I claim peace and happiness, for I know I dwell in the house of the Lord forever.

CONTROL YOUR EMOTIONS

"He that is slow to wrath is of great understanding: but he that is hasty of spirit exalteth folly." I am always poised, serene, and calm. The peace of God floods my mind and my whole being. I practice the Golden Rule and sincerely wish peace and good-will to all men.

I know that the love of all things which are good penetrates my mind casting out all fear. I am now living in the joyous expectancy of the best. My mind is free from all worry and doubt. My words of truth now dissolve every negative thought and emotion with-in me. I forgive everyone; I open the doorway of my heart to God's Presence. My whole being is flooded with the light and understanding from within.

The petty things of life no longer irritate me. When fear, worry, and doubt knock at my door, faith in goodness, truth, and beauty opens the door, and there is no one there. O, God, thou art my God, and there is none else.

PRAYER OF GRATITUDE

"O give thanks unto the Lord; call upon His name; make known His deeds among the people. Sing unto him, sing psalms unto him: talk ye of all his wondrous works. Glory ye in His holy name: let the heart of them rejoice that seek the Lord."

I give thanks sincerely and humbly for all of the goodness, truth, and beauty which flow through me. I have a grateful, uplifted heart for all of the good that has come to me in mind, body, and affairs. I radiate love and goodwill to all mankind. I lift them up in my thought and feeling. I always show my gratitude, and give thanks for all of my blessings. The grateful heart brings my mind and heart in intimate union with the creative Power of the Cosmos. My thankful and exalted state of mind leads me along the ways by which all good things come. "Enter into his gates with thanksgiving, and into his courts with praise: Be thankful unto him, and bless his name."

HOW TO ATTRACT YOUR DIVINE COMPANION

I know that I am one with God now. In Him I live, move, and have my being. God is Life; this life is the life of all men and women. We are all sons and daughters of the one Father.

I know and believe there is a man waiting to love and cherish me. I know I can contribute to his happiness and peace. He loves my ideals, and I love his ideals. He does not want to make me over; neither do

I want to make him over. There is mutual love, freedom, and respect.

There is one mind; I know him now in this mind. I unite now with the qualities and attributes that I admire and want expressed by my husband. I am one with them in my mind. We know and love each other already in Divine Mind. I see the Christ in him; he sees the Christ in me. Having met him within, I must meet him in the without; for this is the law of my own mind.

These words go forth and accomplish whereunto they are sent. I know it is now done, finished, and accomplished in God. Thank you, Father.

HOW TO PRAY FOR COMPANIONSHIP

God is one and indivisible. In Him we love, move, and have our being. I know and believe that God in-dwells every person; I am one with God and with all people. I now attract the right person who is in complete accord with me. This is a spiritual union, because it is the spirit of God functioning through the personality of someone with whom I blend perfectly. I know I can give to this person love, light, and truth. I know I can make this man's life full, complete, and wonderful.

I now decree that he possesses the following qualities and attributes; i.e., he is spiritual, loyal, faithful, and true. He is prosperous, peaceful, and happy. We are irresistibly attracted to each other. Only that which belongs to love, truth, and wholeness can enter my experience. I accept my ideal companion now.

DIVINE FREEDOM

"If ye continue in my word, then are ye my disciples indeed: And ye shall know the truth, and the truth shall make you free." I know the truth, and the truth is that the realization of my desire would free me from all sense of bondage. I accept my freedom; I know it is already established in the Kingdom of God.

I know that all things in my world are projections of my inner attitudes. I am transforming my mind by dwelling on whatsoever things are true, lovely, noble, and Christ-like. I contemplate myself now as possessing all of the good things of Life, such as peace, harmony, health, and happiness.

My contemplation rises to the point of acceptance; I accept the desires of my heart completely. God is the only presence. I am expressing the fullness of God now. I am free! There is peace in my home, heart, and in all of my affairs.

PRAYER FOR PEACE

Peace begins with me. The peace of God fills my mind; the spirit of goodwill goes forth from me to all mankind. God is everywhere, and fills the hearts of all men. In absolute truth all men are now spiritually perfect; they are expressing God's qualities and attributes. These qualities and attributes are Love, Light, Truth, and Beauty.

There are no separate nations. All men belong to the One Country—the One Nation which is God's Country. A country is a dwelling place; I dwell in the secret place of the Most High; I walk and talk with God; so do all men everywhere. There is only One Divine Family, and that is humanity.

There are no frontiers or barriers between nations, because God is One; God is indivisible. God cannot be divided against Himself. The love of God permeates the hearts of all men everywhere. God and His Wisdom rules and guides the nation; He inspires our leaders and the leaders of all nations to do His will, and His will only. The peace of God which passes all understanding fills my mind and the minds of all men throughout the cosmos. Thank you, Father, for Thy peace; it is done.

EXPRESSION

- Predicting My Future
- My Destiny
- Constructive Imagination
- The Balanced Mind
- The Creative Word
- The Answered Prayer
- The Divine Answer
- Divine Guidance
- Right Action
- The Resurrection of My Desire
- Achieving My Goal
- Business Problems
- Principle in Business
- How to Solve Your Problems
- Steps To Success
- The Triumph of Prayer

PREDICTING MY FUTURE

THOU MADEST HIM to have dominion over the works of thy hands. I know that my faith in God determines my future. My faith in God means my faith in all things good. I unite myself now with true ideas, and I know the future will be in the image and likeness of my habitual thinking. "As a man thinketh in his heart so is he." From this moment forward my thoughts are on: "Whatsoever things are true, whatsoever things are honest, whatsoever things are just, whatsoever things are lovely, and of good report;" day and night I meditate on these things, and I know these seeds (thoughts) which I habitually dwell upon will become a rich harvest for me. I am the captain of my own soul; I am the master of my fate; for my thought and feeling are my destiny.

MY DESTINY

I know that I mold, fashion, and create my own destiny. My faith in God is my destiny; this means an abiding faith in all things good. I live in the joy-out expectancy of the best; only the best comes to me. I know the harvest I will reap in the future, because all of my thoughts are God's thoughts, and God is with my thoughts of good. My thoughts are the seeds of goodness, truth, and beauty. I now place my thoughts of love, peace, joy, success, and good-will in the garden of my mind. This is God's garden, and it will yield an abundant harvest. The glory and beauty of God will be expressed in my life. From this moment forward, I express life, love, and truth. I am radiantly happy and prosperous in all ways. Thank you, Father.

CONSTRUCTIVE IMAGINATION

"Those things, which ye have both learned, and received, and heard, and seen in me, do: and the God of peace shall be with you."

My mind is God's Mind, and my thoughts are God's thoughts. This is how I use my imagination daily: I constantly meditate on whatsoever things are true, honest, just, lovely, and of good report; my imagination is the workshop of God at all times. I imagine only peace, harmony, health, wealth, perfect expression, and love. I reject everything unlike God or perfection.

Today I claim my true place in the Kingdom of God. I make it a daily practice to seek first the Kingdom of God within me; then I know that all good things shall be added to me. All of my faith is in God and the good. God's Love is supreme in me, and casts out all fear. I am at peace. I thank you, Father.

THE BALANCED MIND

"Thou wilt keep him in perfect peace whose mind is stayed on thee, because he trusted in thee." I know that the inner desires of my heart come from God within me. God wants me to be happy. The will of God for me is life, love, truth, and beauty. I mentally accept my good now, and I become a perfect, free, flowing channel for the Divine.

I come into His Presence singing; I enter into His courts with praise; I am joyful and happy; I am still and poised.

The Still Small Voice whispers in my ear revealing to me my perfect answer. I am an expression of God. I am always in my true place doing the thing I love to do. I refuse to accept the opinions of man as truth. I now turn within, and I sense and feel the rhythm of the Divine. I hear the melody of God whispering its message of love to me.

My mind is God's mind, and I am always reflecting Divine wisdom and Divine intelligence. My brain symbolizes the Christ capacity to think wisely and spiritually. God's ideas unfold within my mind with perfect sequence. I am always poised, balanced, serene, and calm; for I know that God will always reveal to me the perfect solution to all of my needs.

THE CREATIVE WORD

"Be ye doers of the word, and not hearers only, deceiving your own selves." My creative word is my silent conviction that my prayer is answered. When I speak the word for healing, success, or prosperity, my word is spoken in the consciousness of Life and Power, knowing that it is done. My word has power, because it is one with Omnipotence. The words I speak are always constructive and creative. When I pray, my words are full of life, love, and feeling; this makes my affirmations, thoughts, and words creative. I know the greater my faith behind the word spoken, the more power it has. The words I use form a definite mold, which determine what form my thought is to take. Divine Intelligence operates through me now, and reveals to me what I need to know. I have the answer now. I am at peace. God is Peace.

THE ANSWERED PRAYER

"Before they call, I will answer; and while they are yet speaking, I will hear."

When I pray, I call on the Father, the Son, and the Holy Ghost; the Father is my own consciousness; the Son is my desire; the Holy Ghost is the feeling of being what I want to be.

I now take my attention away from the problem, whatever it may be. My mind and heart are open to the influx from on High.

I know the Kingdom of God is within me. I sense, feel, understand, and know that my own life, my awareness of being, my own I am-ness, is the Living Spirit Almighty. I now turn in recognition to this One Who Forever Is; the Light of God illumines my pathway; I am Divinely inspired and governed in all ways.

Now I begin to pray scientifically in order to bring my desire into manifestation by claiming and feeling myself to be and to have what I long to be and to have. I walk in the inner silent knowing of the soul, because I know my prayer is already answered, as I feel the reality of it in my heart. Thank you, Father; it is done!

THE DIVINE ANSWER

I know that the answer to my problem lies in the God-Self within me. I now get quiet, still, and relaxed. I am at peace. I know God speaks in peace and not in confusion. I am now in tune with the In-finite; I know and believe implicitly that Infinite Intelligence is revealing to me the perfect answer. I think about the solution to my problems. I now live in the mood I would have were my problem solved. I truly live in this abiding faith and trust which is the mood of the solution; this is the spirit of God moving within me. This Spirit is Omnipotent; It is manifesting Itself; my whole being rejoices in the solution; I am glad. I live in this feeling, and give thanks.

I know that God has the answer. With God all things are possible. God is the Living Spirit Almighty within me; He is the source of all wisdom and illumination.

The indicator of the Presence of God within me is a sense of peace and poise. I now cease all sense of strain and struggle; I trust the God-Power implicitly. I know that all the Wisdom and Power I need to live a glorious and successful life are within me. I relax my entire body; I cast all burdens on the Christ; I go free. I claim and feel the Peace of God flooding my mind, heart, and whole being. I know the quiet mind gets its problems solved. I now turn the request over to the God-Presence knowing It has an answer. I am at peace.

DIVINE GUIDANCE

I now dwell on the Omnipresence and Omni action of God. I know that this Infinite Wisdom guides the planets on their source. I know this same Divine Intelligence governs and directs all of my affairs. I claim and believe Divine understanding is mine at all times. I know that all of my activities are controlled by this indwelling Presence. All of my motives are God-like and true. God's wisdom, truth, and beauty are being expressed by me at all times. The All-Knowing One within me knows what to do, and how to do it. My business or profession is completely controlled, governed, and directed by the love of God. Divine guidance is mine. I know God's answer, for my mind is at peace. I rest in the Everlasting Arms.

RIGHT ACTION

I radiate goodwill to all mankind in thought, word, and deed. I know the peace and goodwill that I radiate to my fellowman come back to me a thousand fold. Whatever I need to know comes to me from the God-Self within me. Infinite Intelligence is operating through me revealing to me what I need to know. God in me knows only the answer. The perfect answer is made known to me now. Infinite Intelligence and Divine Wisdom make all decisions through me, and there is only right action and right expression taking place in my life. Every night I wrap myself in the Mantle of God's Love, and fall asleep knowing Divine Guidance is mine. When the dawn comes, I am filled with peace. I go forth into the new day full of faith, confidence, and trust. Thank you, Father.

THE RESURRECTION OF MY DESIRE

My desire for health, harmony, peace, abundance, and security is the voice of God speaking to me. I definitely choose to be happy and successful. I am guided in all ways. I open my mind and heart to the influx of the Holy Spirit; I am at peace. I draw successful and happy people into my experience. I recognize only the Presence and Power of God within me.

The Light of God shines through me and from me into everything about me. The emanation of God's Love flows from me; It is a healing radiance unto everyone who comes into my Presence.

I now assume the feeling of being what I want to be. I know that the way to resurrect my desire is to remain faithful to my ideal, knowing that an Almighty Power is working in my behalf. I live in this mood of faith and confidence; I give thanks that it is done; for it is established in God, and all is well.

ACHIEVING MY GOAL

"In all thy ways acknowledge Him, and He will make plain thy path." My knowledge of God and the way He works is growing by leaps and bounds. I control and direct all of my emotions along peaceful, constructive channels. Divine Love fills all of my thoughts, words, and actions. My mind is at peace; I am at peace with my fellowman. I am always relaxed and at ease. I know that I am here to express God fully in all ways. I believe implicitly in the guidance of the Holy Spirit within. This Infinite Intelligence within me now reveals to me the perfect plan of expression; I move toward it confidently and joyously. The goal and the objective that I have in my mind is good and very good. I have definitely planted in my mind the way of fulfillment. The Al-mighty Power now moves in my behalf; He is a Light on my path.

BUSINESS PROBLEMS

I know and believe my business is God's business; God is my partner in all of my affairs; to me this means His light, love, truth, and inspiration fill my mind and heart in all ways. I solve all of my problems by placing my complete trust in the Divine Power within me. I know that this Presence sustains everything. I now rest in security and peace. This day I am surrounded by perfect understanding; there is a Divine solution to all of my problems. I definitely understand every-one; I am understood. I know that all of my business relationships are in accord with the Divine Law of Harmony. I know that Christ in-dwells all of my customers and clients. I work harmoniously with others to the end that happiness, prosperity, and peace reign supreme.

PRINCIPLE IN BUSINESS

My business is God's business. I am always about my Father's business which is to radiate Life, Love, and Truth to all mankind. I am expressing myself fully now; I am giving of my talents in a wonderful way. I am Divinely compensated.

God is prospering my business, profession, or activity in a wonderful way. I claim that all of those in my organization are spiritual links in its growth, welfare, and prosperity; I know this, believe it, and rejoice that it is so. All of those connected with me are Divinely prospered and illumined by the Light.

The Light that lighteth every man that cometh into the world leads and guides me in all ways. All of my decisions are controlled by Divine Wisdom. Infinite Intelligence reveals better ways in which I can serve humanity. I rest in the Lord forever.

HOW TO SOLVE YOUR PROBLEMS

"What things so ever you desire, when you pray, believe that ye receive them, and ye shall have them." I know that a problem has its solution within it in the form of a desire. The realization of my desire is good and very good. I know and believe that the creative Power within me has the absolute Power to bring forth that which I deeply desire. The Principle which gave me the desire is the Principle which gives it birth. There is absolutely no argument in my mind about this.

I now ride the white horse which is the spirit of God moving upon the waters of my mind. I take my attention away from the problem, and dwell upon the reality of the fulfilled desire. I am using the Law now. I assume the feeling that my prayer is answered. I make it real by feeling the reality of it. In Him I live, move, and have my being; I live in this feeling, and give thanks.

STEPS TO SUCCESS

"Would you not that I be about my Father's business." I know that my business, profession, or activity is God's business. God's business is always basically success-ful. I am growing in wisdom and understanding every day. I know, believe, and accept the fact that God's law of abundance is always working for me, through me, and all around me.

My business or profession is full of right action and right expression. The ideas, money, merchandise, and contacts that I need are mine now and at all times. All of these things are irresistibly attracted to me by the law of universal attraction. God is the life of my business; I am Divinely guided and inspired in all ways. Every day I am presented with wonderful opportunities to grow, expand, and progress. I am building up goodwill. I am a great success, because I do business with others, as I would have them do it with me.

THE TRIUMPH OF PRAYER

I now let go of everything; I enter into the realization of peace, harmony, and joy. God is all, over all, through all, and all in all. I lead the triumphant life, because I know that Divine Love guides, directs, sustains, and heals me. The immaculate Presence of God is at the very center of my being; It is made manifest now in every atom of my body. There can be no delay, impediment, or obstructions to the realization of my heart's desire. The Almighty Power of God is now moving in my behalf. "None shall stay its hand, and say unto it, what doest thou?" I know what I want; my desire is clear-cut and definite. I accept it completely in my mind. I remain faithful to the end. I have entered into Jerusalem; this means my mind is at peace.

The Healing
Power of Your
Subconscious
Mind

The Healing Power of Your Subconscious Mind

Dr. Joseph Murphy

Everyone is definitely concerned with the healing of bodily conditions and human affairs. What is it that heals? Where is this healing power? These are questions asked by everyone. The answer is that this healing power is in the subconscious mind of each person, and a changed mental attitude on the part of the sick person releases this healing power.

No mental or religious science practitioner, psychologist, psychiatrist, or medical doctor ever healed a patient. There is an old saying, "The doctor dresses the wound, but God heals it." The psychologist or psychiatrist proceeds to remove the mental blocks in the patient so that the healing principle may be released, restoring the patient to health. Likewise, the surgeon removes the physical block enabling the healing currents to function normally. No physician, surgeon, or mental science practitioner claims, "he healed the patient." The one healing power is called by many names—Nature, Life, God, Creative Intelligence, and Subconscious Power.

There are many different methods used to remove the mental, emotional, and physical blocks which inhibit the flow of the healing life principle animating all of us. The healing principle resident in your subconscious mind can and will, if properly directed by you or some other person, heal your mind and body of all disease. This healing principle is operative in all men regardless of creed, color, or race. You do not have to belong to some particular church in order to use and participate in this healing process. Your subconscious will heal the burn or cut on your hand even though you profess to be an atheist or agnostic.

The modern mental therapeutic procedure is based on the truth that the infinite intelligence and power of your subconscious mind responds according to your faith. Mental science practitioners or ministers follows the injunction of the Bible. They go into a private place, were still their minds, relax, let go, and think of the infinite healing presence within them. They close their minds to all outside distractions as well as appearances, and then quietly and knowingly turns over a request or desire to the subconscious mind, realizing that the intelligence of the mind will provide answers according to specific needs.

The most wonderful thing to know is this: Imagine the end desired and feel its reality; then the infinite life principle will respond to your conscious choice and your conscious request. This is the meaning of believe you have received, and you shall receive. This is what the modern mental scientist does when practicing prayer therapy.

One process of healing

There is only one universal healing principle operating through everything—the cat, the dog, the tree, the grass, the wind, the earth—for everything is alive. This life principle operates through the animal, vegetable, and mineral kingdoms as instinct and the law of growth. The human mind is consciously aware of this life principle, and can consciously direct it to bless itself in countless ways.

There are many different approaches, techniques, and methods in using the universal power, but there is only one process of healing, which is faith, for according to your faith is it done unto you.

The law of belief

All religions of the world represent forms of belief, and these beliefs are explained in many ways. The law of life is belief. What do you believe about yourself, life, and the universe? It is done unto you as you believe.

Belief is a thought in your mind, which causes the power of your subconscious to be distributed into all phases of your life according to your thinking habits.

You must realize the Bible is not talking about your belief in some ritual, ceremonial, form, institution, or formula. It is talking about belief itself. The belief of your mind is simply the thought of your mind. If thou canst believe, all things are possible to him that believeth (MARK 9:23).

It is foolish to believe in something that will hurt or harm you. Remember, it is not the thing believed in that hurts or harms you, but the belief or thought in your mind that creates the result. All your experiences, all your actions, and all the events and circumstances of your life are but the reflections and reactions to your own thought.

Prayer therapy is the combined function of the conscious and subconscious mind scientifically directed

Prayer therapy is the synchronized, harmonious, and intelligent function of the conscious and subconscious levels of mind specifically directed for a definite purpose. In scientific prayer or prayer therapy, you must know what you are doing and why you are doing it. You trust the law of healing. Prayer therapy is sometimes referred to as mental treatment, or scientific prayer.

In prayer therapy you consciously choose a certain idea, mental picture, or plan which you desire to experience. You realize your capacity to convey this idea or mental image to your subconscious by feeling the reality of the state assumed. As you remain faithful in your mental attitude, your prayer will be answered. Prayer therapy is a definite mental action for a definite specific purpose.

Let's suppose that you decide to heal a certain difficulty by prayer therapy. You are aware that your problem or sickness, whatever it may be, must be caused by negative thoughts charged with fear and lodged in your subconscious mind, and that if you can succeed in cleansing your mind of these thoughts, you will get a healing.

You, therefore, turn to the healing power within your own subconscious mind and remind yourself of its infinite power and intelligence and its capacity to heal all conditions. As you dwell on these truths, your fear will begin to dissolve, and the recollection of these truths also corrects the erroneous beliefs.

You give thanks for the healing that you know will come, and then you keep your mind off the difficulty until you feel guided, after an interval, to pray again. While you are praying, it is essential that you refuse to give any power to any negative conditions or to admit for a second that the healing will not come. This attitude of mind brings about the harmonious union of the conscious and subconscious mind, which releases the healing power.

Faith healing, what it means, and how blind faith works

What is popularly termed faith healing is not the faith mentioned in the Bible, which means a knowledge of the interaction of the conscious and subconscious mind. Faith healers are people who heal without any real scientific understanding of the powers and forces involved. They may claim that they have a special gift of healing, and the sick person's blind belief in these powers may bring results.

Voodoo doctors in primitive societies may heal by incantations, or a person may be healed by touching the so-called bones of saints, or anything else, which cause the patients to honestly believe in the method or process.

Any method which causes one to move from fear and worry to faith and expectancy will heal. There are many persons, who my claim that because a personal theory produces results, it is, therefore, the correct one. This, as already explained in this chapter, cannot be true.

To illustrate how blind faith works: Let's look at the Swiss physician, Franz Anton Mesmer. In 1776 he claimed many cures when he stroked diseased bodies with artificial magnets. Later on he threw away his magnets and evolved the theory of animal magnetism. This he held to be a fluid which pervades the universe, but is most active in the human organism.

He claimed that this magnetic fluid, which was going forth from him to his patients healed them. People flocked to him, and many wonderful cures were affected.

Mesmer moved to Paris, and while there the Government appointed a commission composed of physicians and members of the Academy of Science, of which Benjamin Franklin was a member, to investigate his cures. The report admitted the leading facts claimed by Mesmer, but held that there was no evidence to prove the correctness of his magnetic fluid theory, and said the effects were due to the imagination of the patients.

Soon after this, Mesmer was driven into exile, and died in 1815. Shortly afterwards, Dr. Braid of Manchester undertook to show that magnetic fluid had nothing to do with the production of the healings of Dr. Mesmer. Dr. Braid discovered that patients could be thrown into hypnotic sleep by suggestion, during which many of the well-known phenomena ascribed to magnetism by Mesmer could be produced.

You can readily see that all these cures were undoubtedly brought about by the active imagination of the patients together with a powerful suggestion of health to their subconscious minds. All this could be termed blind faith as there was no understanding in those days as to how the cures were brought about.

Subjective faith and what it means

You will recall the proposition, which need not be repeated at length, that the subjective or subconscious mind of an individual is as amenable to the control of his own conscious or objective mind as it is by the suggestions of another. It follows that whatever may be your objective belief, if you will assume to have faith actively or passively, your subconscious mind will be controlled by the suggestion, and your desire will be fulfilled. The faith required in mental healings is purely subjective.

In the healing of the body it is, of course, desirable to secure the concurrent faith of both the conscious and subconscious mind. However, it is not always essential if you will enter into a state of passivity and receptivity by relaxing the mind and the body and getting into a sleepy state. In this drowsy state your passivity becomes receptive to subjective impression.

Recently, I was asked, "How is it that I got a healing through a minister? I did not believe what he said when he told me that there is no such thing as disease and that matter does not exist."

This man at first thought his intelligence was being insulted, and he protested against such a palpable absurdity. The explanation is simple. He was quieted by soothing words and told to get into a perfectly passive condition, to say nothing, and think of nothing for the time being. His minister also became passive, and affirmed quietly, peacefully, and constantly for about one half hour that this man would have perfect health, peace, harmony, and wholeness. He felt immense relief and was restored to health.

It is easy to see that his subjective faith had been made manifest by his passivity under treatment, and the suggestions of perfect healthfulness by the minister were conveyed to his sub-conscious mind. The two subjective minds were then en rapport. The minister was not handicapped by antagonistic auto-suggestions of the patient arising from objective doubt of the power of the healer or the correctness of the theory. In this sleepy, drowsy state the conscious mind resistance is reduced to a minimum, and results followed. The subconscious mind of the patient being necessarily controlled by such suggestion exercised its functions in accordance therewith, and a healing followed.

The meaning of absent treatment

Suppose you learned that your mother was sick in New York City and you lived in Los Angeles. Your mother would not be physically present where you are, but you could pray for her. (It is the Father within which doeth the work (JOHN 14:10).

The creative law of mind (subconscious mind) serves you and will do the work. Its response to you is automatic. Your treatment is for the purpose of inducing an inner realization of health and harmony in your mentality. This inner realization, acting through the subconscious mind, operates through your mother's subconscious mind as there is but one creative mind. Your thoughts of health, vitality, and perfection operate through the one universal subjective mind, and set a law in motion on the subjective side of life that manifests through her body as a healing.

In the mind principle there is no time or space. It is the same mind that operates through your mother no matter where she may be. In reality there is no absent treatment as opposed to present treatment for the universal mind is omnipresent. You do not try to send out thoughts or hold a thought. Your treatment is a conscious movement of thought, and as you become conscious of the qualities of health, well-being, and relaxation, these qualities will be resurrected in the experience of your mother, and results will follow.

The following is a perfect example of what is called absent treatment. Recently, a listener of our radio program in Los Angeles prayed as follows for her mother in New York who had a coronary thrombosis: "The healing presence is right where my mother is. Her bodily condition is but a reflection of her thought-life like shadows cast on the screen. I know that in order to change the images on the screen I must change the projection reel. My mind is the projection reel, and I now project in my own mind the image of wholeness, harmony, and perfect health for my mother. The infinite healing presence which created my mother's body and all her organs is now saturating every atom of her being, and a river of peace flows through every cell of her body. The doctors are divinely guided and directed, and whoever touches my mother is guided to do the right thing. I know that disease has no ultimate reality; if it had, no one could be healed. I now align myself with the infinite principle of love and life, and I know and decree that harmony, health, and peace are now being expressed in my mother's body."

She prayed in the above manner several times daily, and her mother had a most remarkable recovery after a few days, much to the amazement of her specialist. He complimented her on her great faith in the power of God.

The conclusion arrived at in the daughter's mind set the creative law of mind in motion on the subjective side of life, which manifested itself through her mother's body as perfect health and harmony. What the daughter felt as true about her mother was simultaneously resurrected in the experience of her mother.

Releasing the kinetic action of the subconscious mind

A psychologist friend of mine told me that one of his lungs was infected. X rays and analysis showed the presence of tuberculosis. At night before going to sleep he would quietly affirm, "Every cell, nerve, tissue, and muscle of my lungs are now being made whole, pure, and perfect. My whole body is being restored to health and harmony."

These are not his exact words, but they represent the essence of what he affirmed. A complete healing followed in about a month's time. Subsequent X rays showed a perfect healing.

I wanted to know his method, so I asked him why he repeated the words prior to sleep. Here is his reply, "The kinetic action of the subconscious mind continues throughout your sleep-time period. Hence, give the subconscious mind something good to work on as you drop off into slumber." This was a very wise answer. In thinking of harmony and perfect health, he never mentioned his trouble by name.

I strongly suggest that you cease talking about your ailments or giving them a name. The only sap from which they draw life is your attention and fear of them. Like the above mentioned psychologist, become a mental surgeon. Then your troubles will be cut off like dead branches are pruned from a tree. If you are constantly naming your aches and symptoms, you inhibit the kinetic action, which means the release of the healing power and energy of your subconscious mind. Furthermore, by the law of your own mind, these imaginings tend to take shape, As the thing I greatly feared. Fill your mind with the great truths of life and walk forward in the light of love.

Summary of your aids to health

1. Find out what it is that heals you. Realize that correct directions given to your subconscious mind will heal your mind and body.

2. Develop a definite plan for turning over your requests or desires to your subconscious mind.

3. Imagine the end desired and feel its reality. Follow it through, and you will get definite results.

4. Decide what belief is. Know that belief is a thought in your mind, and what you think you create.

5. It is foolish to believe in sickness and something to hurt or to harm you. Believe in perfect health, prosperity, peace, wealth, and divine guidance.

6. Great and noble thoughts upon which you habitually dwell become great acts.

7. Apply the power of prayer therapy in your life. Choose a certain plan, idea, or mental picture. Mentally and emotionally unite with that idea, and as you remain faithful to your mental attitude, your prayer will be answered.

8. Always remember, if you really want the power to heal, you can have it through faith, which means a knowledge of the working of your conscious and subconscious mind. Faith comes with understanding.

9. Blind faith means that a person may get results in healing without any scientific understanding of the powers and forces involved.

10. Learn to pray for your loved ones who may be ill. Quiet your mind, and your thoughts of health, vitality, and perfection operating through the one universal subjective mind will be felt and resurrected in the mind of your loved one.

ABOUT THE AUTHOR

Joseph Murphy was born on May 20, 1898, in a small town in the County of Cork, Ireland. His father, Denis Murphy, was a deacon and professor at the National School of Ireland, a Jesuit facility. His mother, Ellen, née Connelly, was a housewife, who later gave birth to another son, John, and a daughter, Catherine.

Joseph was brought up in a strict Catholic household. His father was quite devout and, indeed, was one of the few lay professors who taught Jesuit seminarians. He had a broad knowledge of many subjects and developed in his son the desire to study and learn.

Ireland at that time was suffering from one of its many economic depressions, and many families were starving. Although Denis Murphy was steadily employed, his income was barely enough to sustain the family.

Young Joseph was enrolled in the National School and was a brilliant student. He was encouraged to study for the priesthood and was accepted as a Jesuit seminarian. However, by the time he reached his late teen years, he began to question the Catholic orthodoxy of the Jesuits, and he withdrew from the seminary. Since his goal was to explore new ideas and gain new experiences—a goal he could not pursue in Catholic-dominated Ireland—he left his family to go to America.

He arrived at the Ellis Island Immigration Center with only $5 in his pocket. His first project was to find a place to live. He was fortunate to locate a rooming house where he shared a room with a pharmacist who worked in local drugstore.

Joseph's knowledge of English was minimal, as Gaelic was spoken both in his home and at school, so like most Irish immigrants, Joseph worked as a day laborer, earning enough to keep fed and housed.

He and his roommate became good friends, and when a job opened up at the drugstore where his friend worked, he was hired to be an assistant to the pharmacist. He immediately enrolled in a school to study pharmacy. With his keen mind and desire to learn, it didn't take long before Joseph passed the qualification exams and became a full-fledged pharmacist. He now made enough money to rent his own apartment. After a few years, he purchased the drugstore, and for the next few years ran a successful business.

When the United States entered World War II, Joseph enlisted in the Army and was assigned to work as a pharmacist in the medical unit of the 88th Infantry Division. At that time, he renewed his interest in religion and began to read extensively about various religious beliefs. After his discharge from the Army, he chose not to return to his career in pharmacy. He traveled extensively, taking courses in several universities both in the United States and abroad.

From his studies, Joseph became enraptured by the various Asian religions and went to India to learn about them in depth. He studied all of the major religions from the time of their beginning. He extended these studies to the great philosophers from ancient times until the present.

Although he studied with some of the most intelligent and far-sighted professors, the one person who most influenced Joseph was Dr. Thomas Troward, who was a judge as well as a philosopher, doctor, and professor. Judge Troward became Joseph's mentor. From him he not only learned philosophy, theology, and law, but also was introduced to mysticism and particularly, the Masonic order. He became an active member of this order and over the years rose in the Masonic ranks to the 32nd degree in the Scottish Rite.

Upon his return to the United States, Joseph chose to become a minister and bring his broad knowledge to the public. As his concept of Christianity was not traditional and indeed ran counter to most of the Christian denominations, he founded his own church in Los Angeles. He attracted a small number of congregants, but it did not take long for his message of optimism and hope rather than the "sin and damnation" sermons of so many ministers to attract many men and women to his church.

Dr. Joseph Murphy was a proponent of the New Thought movement. This movement was developed in the late 19th and early 20th centuries by many philosophers and deep thinkers who studied this phenomenon and preached, wrote, and practiced a new way of looking at life. By combining a metaphysical, spiritual, and pragmatic approach to the way we think and live, they uncovered the secret of attaining what we truly desire.

The proponents of the New Thought movement preached a new idea of life that brings out new methods and more perfected results, and we have the power to use it to enrich our lives. We can do all these things only as we have found the law and worked out the understanding of the law, which God seemed to have written in riddles in the past.

Of course, Dr. Murphy wasn't the only minister to preach this positive message. Several churches, whose ministers and congregants were influenced by the New Thought movement, were founded and developed in the decades following World War II. The Church of Religious Science, the Unity Church, and similar places of worship preach philosophies similar to this. Dr. Murphy named his organization The Church of Divine Science. He often shared platforms, conducted joint programs with his similar-thinking colleagues, and trained other men and women to join their ministry.

Over the years, other churches joined with him in developing an organization called the Federation of Divine Science, which acts an umbrella for all Divine Science churches. Each of the Divine Science church leaders continues to push for more education, and Dr. Murphy was one of the leaders to support the creation of the Divine Science School in St. Louis, Missouri, to train new ministers and provide ongoing educational education for both ministers and congregants.

The annual meeting of the Divine Science ministers was a must to attend, and Dr. Murphy was a featured speaker at them. He encouraged the participants to study and continue to learn, particularly about the importance of the subconscious mind.

Over the next few years, Murphy's local Church of Divine Science grew so large that his building was too small to hold them. He rented The Wilshire Ebell Theater, a former movie theater. His services were so well attended that even this venue could not always accommodate all who wished to attend. Classes conducted by Dr. Murphy and his staff supplemented his Sunday services that were attended by 1,300 to 1,500 people. These were supplemented by seminars and lectures that were held most days and evenings. The church remained at the Wilshire Ebell Theater in Los Angeles until 1976, when it moved to a new location in Laguna Hills, California, near a retirement community.

To reach the vast numbers of people who wanted to hear his message, Dr. Murphy created a weekly radio talk show, which eventually reached an audience of over a million listeners.

Many of his followers wanted more than just summaries and suggested that he tape his lectures and radio programs. He was at first reluctant to do so, but agreed to experiment. His radio programs were recorded on extra-large 78rpm discs, a common practice at that time. He had six cassettes made from one of these discs and placed them on the information table in the lobby of the Wilshire Ebell Theater. They sold out the first hour. This started a new venture. His

tapes of his lectures explaining biblical texts, and pro-
viding meditations and prayers for his listeners were
not only sold in his church, but in other churches,
bookstores, and via the mail.

As the church grew, Dr. Murphy added a staff of
professional and administrative personnel to assist
him in the many programs in which he was involved
and in researching and preparing his first books. One
of the most effective members of his staff was his
administrative secretary, Dr. Jean Wright. The working relationship developed into a romance, and they
were married—a lifelong partnership that enriched
both of their lives.

At this time (the 1950s), there were very few major
publishers of spiritually inspired material. The Murphys located some small publishers in the Los Angeles
area, and with them produced a series of small books
(often 30 to 50 pages printed in pamphlet form) that
were sold, mostly in churches, from $1.50 to $3.00 per
book. When the orders for these books increased to
the point where they required second and third print-
ings, major publishers recognized that there was a mar-
ket for such books and added them to their catalogs.

Dr. Murphy became well known outside of the
Los Angeles area as a result of his books, tapes, and
radio broadcasts and was invited to lecture all over
the country. He did not limit his lectures to religious

matters, but spoke on the historical values of life, the art of wholesome living, and on the teachings of great philosophers—both from the Western and Oriental cultures.

As Dr. Murphy never learned to drive, he had to arrange for somebody to drive him to the various places where he was invited to lecture and other places in his very busy schedule. One of Jean's functions as his administrative secretary and later as his wife was to plan his assignments, arrange for trains or flights, airport pickups, hotel accommodations, and all the other details of the trips.

The Murphys traveled frequently to many countries around the world. One of his favorite working vacations was to hold seminars on cruise ships. These trips were for a week or more and would take him to many countries around the world.

One of Dr. Murphy's most rewarding activities was speaking to the inmates at many prisons. Many ex-convicts wrote him over the years, telling him how his words had truly turned their lives around and inspired them to live spiritual and meaningful lives.

He toured the United States and many countries in Europe and Asia. In his lectures, he emphasized the importance of understanding the power of the subconscious mind and the life principles based on belief in the one God, the "I AM."

Dr. Murphy's pamphlet-sized books were so popular that he began to expand them into more detailed and longer works. His wife gave us some insight into his manner and method of writing. She reported that he wrote his manuscripts on a tablet and pressed so hard on his pencil or pen that you could read the page by the imprint on the next page. He seemed to be in a trance while writing. His writing style was to remain in his office for four to six hours without disturbance until he stopped and said that was enough for the day. Each day was the same. He never went back into the office again until the next morning to finish what he'd started. He took no food or drink while he was working, He was just alone with his thoughts and his huge library of books, to which he referred from time to time. His wife sheltered him from visitors and calls and kept things moving for church business and other activities.

Dr. Murphy was always looking for a simple way to discuss the issues and to elaborate points that would explain in detail how it affects the individual. He chose some of his lectures to present on cassettes, records, or CDs, as the technologies developed and new methods entered the audio field.

His entire work of CDs and cassettes are tools that can be used for most problems that individuals encounter in life, and have been time-tested to accomplish the goals as intended. His basic theme is that the solution to problems lies within oneself. Outside elements cannot change one's thinking. That is, your mind is your own. To live a better life, it's your mind not outside circumstances, that you must change. You create your own destiny. The power of change is in your mind, and by using the power of your subconscious mind, you can make those changes for the better.

Dr. Murphy wrote more than 30 books. His most famous work, *The Power of Your Subconscious Mind*, which was first published in 1963, became an immediate bestseller. It was acclaimed as one of the best self-help guides ever written. Millions of copies have been sold and continue to be sold all over the world.

Among some of his other best-selling books were *Telepsychics—The Magic Power of Perfect Living, The Amazing Laws of Cosmic Mind, Secrets of the I-Ching, The Miracle of Mind Dynamics, Your Infinite Power to Be Rich,* and *The Cosmic Power Within You.*

Dr. Murphy died in December 1981, and his wife, Dr. Jean Murphy, continued his ministry after his death. In a lecture she gave in 1986, quoting her late husband, she reiterated his philosophy:

I want to teach men and women of their Divine Origin, and the powers regnant within them. I want to inform that this power is within and that they are their own saviors and capable of achieving their own salvation. This is the message of the Bible and nine-tenths of our confusion today is due to wrongful, literal interpretation of the life-transforming truths offered in it.

I want to reach the majority, the man on the street, the woman overburdened with duty and suppression of her talents and abilities. I want to help others at every stage or level of consciousness to learn of the wonders within.

She said of her husband: "He was a practical mystic, possessed by the intellect of a scholar, the mind of a successful executive, the heart of the poet. His message summed up was: "You are the king, the ruler of your world for you are one with God."

Printed in the USA
CPSIA information can be obtained
at www.ICGtesting.com
JSHW05195815O824
68134JS00056B/3013

9 781722 502799